The
BALSAMIC
VINEGAR
Cookbook

By Meesha Halm

Photography by Noel Barnhurst

CollinsPublishersSanFrancisco
A Division of HarperCollinsPublishers

FIRST PUBLISHED IN USA 1996
by Collins Publishers San Francisco
1160 Battery Street, San Francisco, CA 94111-1213
HarperCollins Web Site: http://www.harpercollins.com

COPYRIGHT © 1996 HARPERCOLLINS PUBLISHERS INC.

Text: Meesha Halm
Recipe Development: Rick Rodgers
Photograhy: Noel Barnhurst
Photograher's Assistants: Jamie Hadley
              and Shelley Ward
Food Stylist: Karletta Moniz
Food Stylist Assitant: Kelly Jones
Design: Lisa Schulz/Elysium Design
              Shelly Meadows/Homefire
Illustration: David Danz

LIBRARY OF CONGRESS
CATALOGING-IN-PUBLICATION DATA
Halm, Meesha
The balsamic vinegar cookbook / by Meesha Halm;
photgraphy by Noel Barnhurst.
  p. cm.
Includes index.
ISBN 0-00-225133-7
I. Cookery (Vinegar) I. Title.
TX819. V5H34 1996
641.6'2--dc20
96-5389
CIP

PRINTED IN CHINA
10 9 8 7 6 5 4 3

ACKNOWLEDGMENTS
*Many thanks to all people who assisted me in the research and
creation of this book, particularly Paul Bertolli, Rick Rodgers and
Gianni salvaterra. Additional thanks to Richard Rogers, Paul Farber,
Maria Livia Manicardi, Darrell Corti, Matt Buckman, Jon Fox,
Victoria Kalish, Shelly Meadows, Lisa Schulz, Terri Driscoll,
Kristen Wurz, Jenny Collins, Kathy Poyma, Jennifer Ward,
Noel Barnhurst and Karletta Moniz. Finally, I am also indebted to
two exceptional books,* The Splendid Table *by Lynne Rosetto Kasper*
and The Treasures of the Italian Table *by Burton Anderson,*
*which provided me with invaluable informatio on the history and
significance of aceto balsamico tradizionale.*

Contents

⬩—◆—⬩

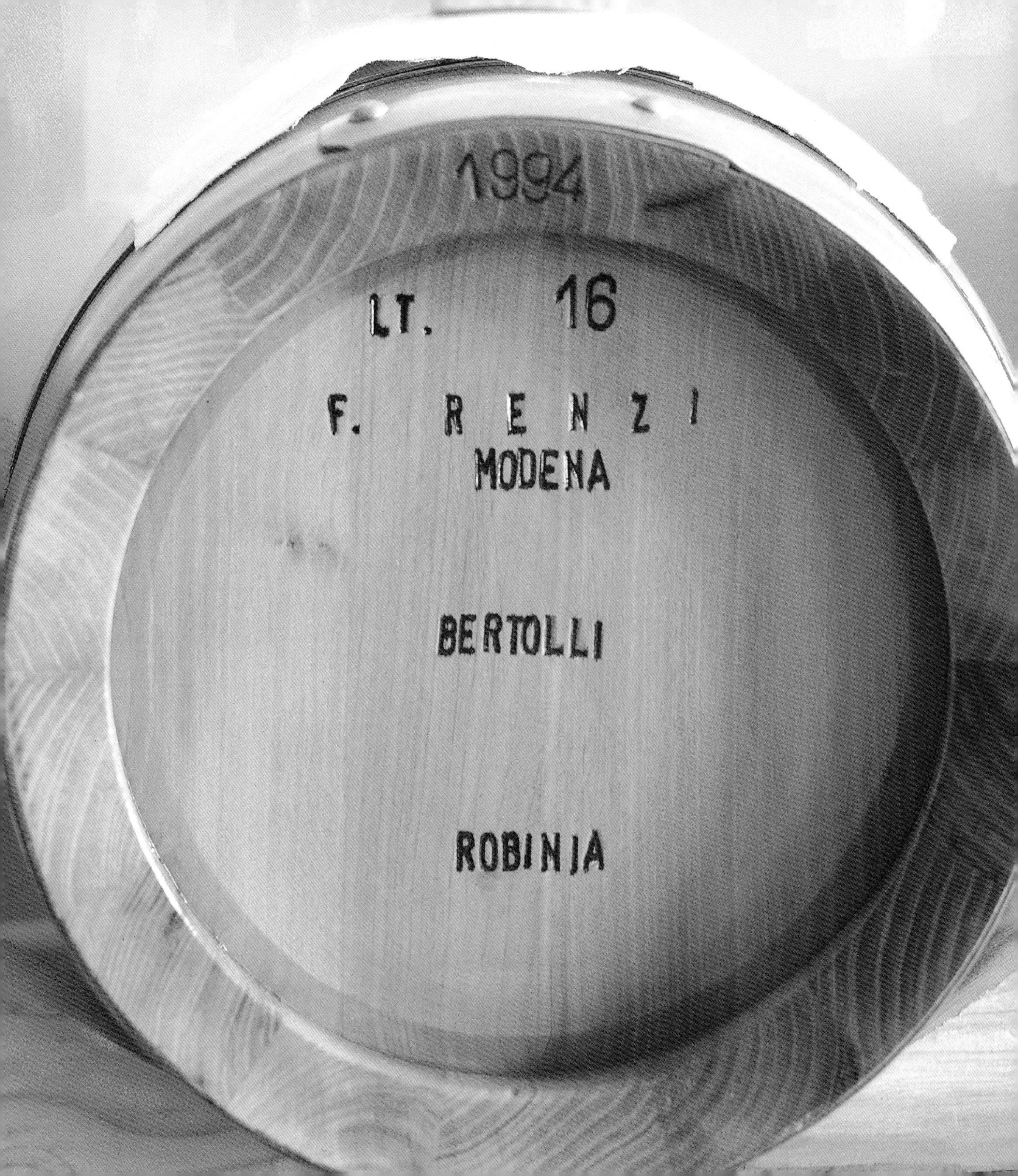
1994
LT. 16
F. RENZI
MODENA
BERTOLLI
ROBINJA

INTRODUCTION

Balsamic vinegar has taken the cooking world by storm. This viscous, sweet-and-sour brown vinegar that hails from the Emilia-Romagna region of Italy is a featured attraction at trendy restaurants, in gourmet food magazines, and on supermarket shelves across the globe. Most people, however, would be surprised to learn that they have never tasted authentic balsamic vinegar.

THE HISTORY OF BALSAMIC VINEGAR

Until 25 years ago, true balsamic vinegar, or *aceto balsamico tradizionale* as it is called in Italian, was an artisanal product relatively unknown outside of Italy. Wealthy families in the small towns of Modena and Reggio in the Emilia-Romagna region, just west of Bologna, had been making the rare condiment for nearly a thousand years, but never for commercial use. Instead, families would care for their supply over the years, passing it on as an heirloom, giving it away in small vials to esteemed friends, or bequeathing it to a daughter as part of her dowry.

Authentic balsamic vinegar has a very rich cultural and culinary history, steeped in superstition, legend, and politics. Long revered for its curative properties, balsamic vinegar derives its name from the word *balm* (rooted in the Latin *balsamum*), which refers to an aromatic resin or odor, as well as an agency that soothes, relieves, or heals. According to Lynne Rossetto Kasper in *The Splendid Table*, it has been credited with everything from warding off evil spirits to stimulating the appetite, restoring tranquility, curing colds, treating heart conditions, preventing insomnia, and soothing throat inflammations. The practice of making a sweet condiment from boiled-down grape juice dates back to ancient times, when the Romans made a mixture called *sapa*. In *The Pleasures of the Italian Table,* Burton Anderson traces the making of refined wood-aged vinegars in Emilia-Romagna back to the 11th century, when it was a duchy ruled by the Este family. In the late Middle Ages and Renaissance, the ruling class enjoyed these vinegars as a refined drink, which they believed to be a remedy for the plague. But it wasn't until the 18th century, when the Este family moved its dominion from Ferrara to Modena, that the term *balsamico* came to refer to the region's local specialty vinegars aged in wood. By the 19th century, balsamico had reached commodity status. Heads of states from Paris to Moscow knew Modena's Archduke Francesco IV for his *aceto del duca,* which he gave as a symbol of friendship. When his son was finally ousted at the end of the Este family reign, he supposedly managed to escape with supplies of the beloved elixir.

After that, aceto balsamico sank into obscurity, a secret to the rest of the world and relatively unknown even to other Italians. However, it continued to be an integral part of the fabric of life in the small towns of Modena and Reggio, where its making was akin to an art form. In his many books on the subject, balsamic vinegar expert Renato Bergonzini refers to the symbolic nature of balsamico. New barrels were started at the birth of a child and given away at weddings. Families would cherish their reserve, passed down through generations, giving away century-old vinegars only as a special gift to treasured friends, visiting dignitaries, and doctors. Stashed in the attic, slowly maturing into liquid gold despite the frenetic activity of life down below, balsamic vinegar came to be considered a symbol of peace.

THE MAKING OF ACETO BALSAMICO TRADIZIONALE

A great mystique enshrouds the making of authentic balsamic vinegar. An old saying in Modena contends, "Who will first start the vinegar will not taste it, but his children and grandchildren will." Although prepared according to time-honored methods, the specific details of the process have varied over the years, and every family carefully guards its secret recipe. A treatise from the 1800s on the art of vinegar making states, "Beyond these barrels and Trebbiano grapes, all you need is time." In truth, it is not so simple.

The production of balsamic vinegar resembles that of wine making. It begins with the unfermented juice of local grapes, traditionally, the white Trebbiano, although other varietals, such as the white Occhio di Gatto and Spergola and the red Berzemino and Lambrusco, are permitted. The grapes, picked at the peak of ripeness, are crushed and then pressed into a juice called *mosto.* (Often, if the sugar level in the grapes is too low, the grapes are put out in wooden boxes and left in the sun for further ripening before crushing.) The must is then cooked down in open pots over a direct flame and simmered for 24 to 30 hours, until it becomes an intensely sweet concentrate, reduced in volume by one-half or more. During the long simmering, the grapes' sugars caramelize slightly, giving the liquid an amber hue. This unfermented juice, called *mosto cotto,* is then cooled, allowed to settle, and, in accordance with traditional methods, transferred to a *batteria* (a set of progressively smaller wooden barrels). The liquid is then stored in vinegar attics, called *acetaie,* generally on the top floor of the house, to ferment, evaporate, and age over a minimum of 12 years and often decades, until it becomes a complex, aromatic, intensely sweet, syrupy condiment.

Balsamic vinegar undergoes a long and complex aging process, in which it is transferred into a series of progressively smaller barrels made of different woods called a batteria.

There is no set number of barrels required for a batteria, but a minimum of three are needed for the mosto cotto to undergo the processes that give balsamic vinegar its complex character— *trasformazione* (transformation), *maturazione* (maturation), and *invecchiamento* (aging). The barrels, which range in capacity from 100 to 10 liters, are fashioned from hard and soft woods such as ash, oak, juniper, mulberry, chestnut, and cherry. Each barrel imparts flavor and color to the mosto cotto, resulting in a vinegar with a multilayered character. The kinds of woods employed and their position in the series varies widely among producers, typically dictated by personal preference and economic viability, as well as the wood's density, porosity, flavor, and availability. Some producers prefer to use stronger, more aromatic woods for the small casks at the end of the series to impart a sharper finishing character to the vinegar in the final stages. Others favor the more neutral woods, which allow the vinegar to mellow. All barrels are highly porous and have large square bungholes covered by a cotton cloth to allow maximum exposure to air and assist in evaporation.

Balsamic vinegar goes through two steps of transformation: alcoholic fermentation and acetic oxidation. Fermentation takes place either in the batteria or in large storage tanks or barrels. The cooked must is added to the tanks or barrels, along with either an acetobacter, called the mother, or a small amount of strong wine vinegar. Yeasts, either introduced or allowed to develop spontaneously, convert the natural sugars found in the must into alcohol, which is in turn consumed by the acetobacters and converted into vinegar. Traditionally, this process is begun in late summer, when the heat encourages a greater rate of bacterial activity.

The vinegar, if it has been fermented in tanks or barrels, is then transferred to the batteria where the barrels are filled 66 to 75 percent of capacity (leaving space for further acetic oxidation to occur). Over the course of a year, anywhere from 15 percent to 30 percent of the volume is lost through evaporation. Every year, each barrel is topped off from the next larger one, and the largest is replenished with new cooked must. This topping-up step is called *rincalzo.* The shuttling from cask to cask is called *travaso* (*tra* means between, and *vasi* means barrels). Rincalzo is typically done during the coldest part of the year, when bacterial activity is low. Also at this time, the by-products of the fermentation precipitate, leaving a clear liquid on top. Unlike with wine, extreme fluctuations in temperature actually benefit balsamic vinegar, helping it achieve its density and complex character. Modena and Reggio, with their hot summer evenings and cool winter nights, have an ideal climate for vinegar attics.

Over the years, the vinegar is transferred into smaller and smaller barrels, the water in it evaporates and the vinegar mellows, becoming viscous, intensely aromatic, and sweet. The vinegar's final balance is achieved through a series of corrections made periodically to adjust the sugar or acidity level, a task that requires a great deal of skill and expertise on the part of the vinegar maker. When the vinegar has passed through each barrel, it is transferred to tiny barrels or open barrels for further maturing. Law requires a minimum of 12 years of aging before the vinegar can be considered for approval and sold as aceto balsamico tradizionale. It is not unusual, however, for producers to draw off small portions sooner for personal use.

Over the years, the barrels build up deposits that impart complex flavors to the vinegar as it passes through them. These deposits, called *umificazione*—but commonly referred to as the "patrimony" of the vinegar—consist of precipitates, used-up yeasts, bits of wood that have rubbed free, and other by-products; They make the old barrels so valuable that when the barrels begin to deteriorate, new wood is built up around them in a process called *rivestimento.*

Every step in the process—from the concentration and slight caramelization of the grape juice to the fermentation and oxidation, the constant evaporation, and the 12 years housed in different woods—contributes to balsamic vinegar's layers of sweetness, sourness, earthiness, and intensity. Naturally, this comes at a price, since the yields on traditional production are extremely low. After being cooked down and allowed to evaporate for 12 years, only a fraction of the original volume remains by the time the vinegar is ready for bottling. In fact, 800 gallons of grape must yield about 30 gallons of balsamic vinegar. This explains why a 3-ounce bottle of aceto balsamico tradizionale can cost more than $100.

THE ADVENT OF COMMERCIAL VINEGARS

The commercialization of balsamic vinegar began after World War II, but didn't really explode until the late 1970s when chefs in Italy discovered that its intense flavors complemented the newly emergent cooking style. Foreigners traveling in Italy discovered it on their visits, and awareness of the rare vinegar grew at a staggering pace. Unfortunately, local families simply could not make enough. In order to meet the new demand, many producers developed imitation versions. By the late 1970s, the annual sales of cheap commercial balsamic vinegar had reached an estimated 1.75 million liters, as compared to only 1,760 liters of the approved tradizionale.

In an effort to thwart the flood of commercial vinegars, traditional producers from Modena and Reggio waged a campaign to distinguish themselves from their imitators. In the ensuing years, a fierce rivalry between the two towns developed, each town claiming to be the exclusive authority on the venerated vinegar. In 1987, after a long fight, the provinces of Modena and Reggio were granted dual Domain of Control (DOC). Today, only vinegars that conform to a decree written by the Ministry of Agriculture can be called aceto balsamico tradizionale, with consortiums in Modena and Reggio overseeing the certification and bottling of authentic balsamico.

To receive the consortium seal and bear the words *Aceto Balsamico Tradizionale*, vinegars must have been made in the traditional artisanal method, been aged for a minimum of 12 years, and been produced in the provinces of Modena or Reggio. No wine vinegar or caramel can be added. Producers must bring their vinegar before a board of five expert tasters and pass tests for color, density, aroma, and taste. Only one-third of the vinegar submitted wins approval, which must be unanimous. Once the vinegar has been accepted, it is bottled in the presence of the producer and consortium members into distinctive 100-milliliter bottles bearing the producer's label and the consortium's seal of guarantee.

BALSAMIC VINEGAR TODAY

Commercial vinegars, referred to disparagingly as *industriale* in Italy, make up more than 99 percent of today's market. In recent years, however, consumers familiar only with imitation brands have become more knowledgeable about authentic balsamic vinegar. As a result, sales of aceto balsamico tradizionale have increased. According to Gianni Salvaterra, spokesperson for the consortium of Modena, in 1987, its first year, the consortium bottled 4,000 100-milliliter bottles. By 1995, less than a decade later, approved production had soared to 10,000 bottles.

Ironically, despite the protracted battle to win DOC for the region, many modern balsamic producers eschew the ancient methods of their forebearers and bypass the consortium approval process altogether. This younger generation of producers, many of whom have inherited the family acetaia, are experimenting with ways of developing a rich, complex vinegar in a shorter time. Combining old and new methods, they follow the traditional fermentation and aging, but they manipulate the means of production and often sell their vinegar at a younger age. This way they subsidize the enormous expense of housing 12-, 25-, and 50-year-old vinegars. Many produce vinegars that would qualify for consortium approval but feel that the tradizionale market is too limited and prefer to sell their vinegar under a different name. At prices ranging from $16 to $30 per 250 milliliters, these vinegars are what savvy Italians use and what the rest of us who balk at paying $100 or more for vinegar can enjoy.

Every year, the Consorteria dell'Aceto Balsamico Naturale di Spilamberto, an association of 1,200 vinegar producers and devotees that trains the tasters for the other two consortia, hosts the Palio di San Giovanni in which producers enter their best balsamic vinegars to be judged. Dressed in formal regalia of caps and gowns, the master tasters, who have undergone rigorous courses to certify their mastery of vinegar appreciation, swirl and sample more than 1,200 vinegars, then grade them with a maximum score of 400 points. (A score of 250 qualifies a vinegar as aceto balsamico tradizionale.) In 1991, Sante Bertoni, one of the neotraditional producers, received a score of 341, causing quite a stir and portending a new era in aceto balsamico.

HOW TO SELECT
BALSAMIC VINEGAR

◆—◆—◆

The balsamic vinegar that most consumers are familiar with, that is, the kind found in supermarkets, is not authentic. For most people, however, spending over $100 for 3 ounces of vinegar is simply not an option. Luckily, it is possible to enjoy the flavors of balsamic vinegar at a reasonable price, although finding a good commercial brand can be a bit of a challenge. The dizzying number of balsamic vinegars on the market reflects an enormous range in taste, quality, and price. Bottles of balsamic vinegar can fetch as little as $4 for 750 milliliters or as much as $535 for a 3-ounce bottle dating from 1650. Some are sweet, viscous, and woody; others bitter, overly acidic, or caramel-tasting. Unfortunately, bottles lined up neatly on a shelf offer few clues. Although authentic balsamico has a sign of approval and the consortium crest on the label (and at $100 and up for 3 ounces, it is hardly difficult to recognize), the bulk of vinegars claiming to be *aceto balsamico di Modena* are simply impostors.

Aging is often a criterion used for judging fine balsamic vinegars, although determining the age from a label can be difficult at best. According to ministerial decrees, it is illegal to print the age of the vinegar on the label. However, many vinegar labels do make such claims, and here again, the information can be misleading. A "10-year-old" vinegar can mean that any amount, even an eyedropper full, of older vinegar was added to the end product, or that the starter must

was begun 10 years ago. Ultimately, it is the taste, not the age, that determines the quality of a vinegar.

TYPES OF BALSAMIC VINEGAR

◆—◆—◆

There is a great deal of controversy and confusion over the categorization of balsamic vinegar. While legal and emotional battles dictate the use of names, the best distinctions are on how the vinegar is made. Loosely speaking, there are three styles of vinegars on the market today: artisan-style, industriale, and imitation.

ARTISAN-STYLE: The best known of this style are *aceto balsamico tradizionale di Modena* and *aceto balsamico tradizionale di Reggio Emilia.* This is the authentic vinegar, made in the traditional artisan-style in the provinces of Modena and Reggio as it has been made for 1,000 years, and which has been tested and approved by the balsamic consortiums of Modena and Reggio. Look for the word *tradizionale* on the label. Approved vinegars can also be identified by their distinctive bottle. For Modena, the approved bottle, designed by Italian stylist Giorgetto Giugiaro, is a small bulbous globe on a rectangular base, made out of one piece of glass. Color capsules indicate age; white denotes a younger vinegar; gold an extra vecchio, a very old one. Modenese consortium tasters prefer the characteristics of older vinegars—hence, their average tradizionale is 20 to 30 years old.

The Reggiano consortium certifies three levels of aceto balsamico tradizionale vinegars—*tradizionale, qualitá superiore,* and the highest, *extra vecchio*—

each indicated by foiled and stamped color labels. These sell for roughly $75 for the red tradizionale label, $115 for the silver qualità superiore, and $175 for the gold extra vecchio. All three come in a curvaceous vase-shaped bottle with a round seal that states Consortium of Producers of Aceto Balsamico Tradizionale di Reggio Emilia. Reggio is often attacked by its Modenese neighbors for what they claim is a lenient grading system. Indeed, Reggio's tradizionale vinegars tend to have a sweeter, more plummy flavor than their Modenese counterparts.

In fact, because different barrels are used over the years and the vinegar is always a blend of old and new, no two bottles of tradizionale are alike. Even among producers, there are variations in age and style. However, certain characteristics don't change. Fine tradizionales are thick, luscious, dark purplish brown, and aromatic, with sweet-and-sour notes in a harmonious blend. When you tip the bottle, the vinegar should coat the sides of the glass. The vinegars taste of everything from old port, toffee, vanilla, caramel, and chocolate to plum jam, resinous wood, and herbs such as rosemary and thyme. Their initial sweetness is followed by a slight acidity. Because of their intense viscosity and flavor, tradizionales are meant to be used sparingly. The consortiums of Modena and Reggio provide booklets with every bottle of tradizionale that feature recipes that use the authentic vinegar.

There is also a newly emergent category of artisan-style balsamic vinegar. These vinegars are made by producers who use only unadulterated cooked grape must and follow traditional artisan methods, but sell a portion of their supplies sooner than the legally required 12 years, or by small producers who make vinegars that could qualify for the tradizionale category, but do not want to pay the consortium membership fee or the bottling fee. Since these vinegars do not go through the consortium's approval process, by law they are not allowed to be called *tradizionale.* Instead, they are often marketed as *condimenti* (or *salsa*) but differ from the industrially produced blended vinegars that also go by that name. Although quite popular in Italy, only small amounts of these vinegars are exported. Producers of these artisan-style vinegars, who take offense at the label "industriale," as they are often referred to in Italy, are trying to get a special categorization for their products.

Although they are still expensive, anywhere from $16 to $50 for 250 milliliters, these artisan-style condimenti vinegars are a bargain compared to the real tradizionale. Recommended producers are Bertoni Sante, Roberto and Giovanni Cavalli, Sereni Pier Luigi, and Manicardi. There are also a number of American producers in California making balsamicos in this fashion.

INDUSTRIALE: There is a wide range of industrially produced vinegars available on the market. Often packaged in beautiful shapely bottles, these vinegars vary greatly in flavor, quality, and price. The process by which the vinegar is made, rather than

the name or the packaging, is what is important to discern a good-quality vinegar. Typically, these vinegars do not follow the time-intensive methods of tradizionale, are a mixture of vinegar and other components, and are produced on a much larger scale. The best are marketed by the names condimenti, salad mix, seasoning, or *da condire.* Some are high-quality artisan-style blends, made from cooked grape must and aged wine vinegar; others blend very old wine vinegar with a small percentage of tradizionale and are aged in barrels for a short period. Some have even had wood chips thrown into the vats.

The most popular of the industrially produced vinegars, which make up the majority of the market, are labeled *aceto balsamico di Modena.* Check the labels for API MO and API RE, indicating that the vinegars were actually made in Modena or Reggio. Others come from regions as distant as Naples or New Jersey and are simply imitations.

Industriale vinegars, even those of the highest quality, should never be confused with the authentic aceto balsamico tradizionale. At their best, they are less complex facsimiles. They are straightforward and acidic and best used to blend into soups, stews, and salads.

Most experts agree that you get what you pay for. Generally, the more expensive the industriale vinegar, the better the quality. However, some higher-priced vinegars taste no better than supermarket varieties. Recommended commercial producers are Cattani, Grosoli, Federzoni, Giusti, Fini, Fiorucci, and Manicardi. In addition to their own labels, their vinegar is sold under other labels, such as Antiqua, Cibo di Lidia Aceto Balsamico di Modena, Compagna del Montale Aceto Balsamico di Modena, and Masserie di Sant'Erame Balsamic Vinegar of Modena.

Every vinegar has slightly different characteristics: Some have a tangy sweet-and-sour bite, others a woody flavor, others a viscous, syrupy consistency. Whatever its attributes, a vinegar's flavors should meld harmoniously. The best advice is to buy from a reputable source, sample as many different vinegars as you can, and choose according to your personal taste.

IMITATION: These vinegars are not made according to the traditional methods, and are generally produced outside Modena and Reggio. Nonetheless, many are marketed as aceto balsamico di Modena. Such imitations make up at least two-thirds of the balsamic vinegar market. These vinegars do not contain any amount of balsamic or cooked grape must and are usually red wine vinegar cut with water. Since no fermentation or oxidation takes place, they can be made in a day. Cane sugar, caramel, vanilla, and/or herbs are added to fake sweetness and depth.

In 1993, the agriculture ministry issued a decree that sought to restrict the geographical reference to Modena or Reggio, but the criteria are still quite vague. There is raging controversy about this categorization in Italy, with producers and politicians disagreeing on who can claim the use of the geographical reference. To confuse matters, there is talk of the European Union imposing the name aceto balsamico di Modena on all non-tradizionale products in an attempt to standardize their trade policies.

Another product to be wary of is so-called white balsamic vinegar, which boasts that no caramel or artificial colorings have been added. This vinegar is entirely inauthentic. In fact, coloring is never added to real balsamic vinegar. The toasty brown of tradizionale comes from the natural caramelization of the grape must and from time spent in wood barrels.

COOKING TIPS

❖

A document in the Estes ducal archives reveals that as early as 1556, balsamic vinegars were classified into types ranging from *da agresto* (sour) to *per cucina* (for cooking) to *da tavola* (for the table) to *per gentiluomini* (for gentlemen). In Italy today, however, vinegars are often distinguished by age as *giovane* (young; 3 to 5 years), *medio corpo* (medium-bodied; 16 to 20 years), and *il patriarca* (older than 20 years), and used accordingly.

Balsamic vinegar is still a rarity in most parts of Italy and is not used as liberally as in other countries. In 1995, more than 80 percent of production was exported, mainly to Germany, Switzerland, France, the United States, Canada, and Japan. Considered more a condiment or seasoning than a vinegar, it is used sparingly by Italian cooks. Although exorbitantly expensive, a little bit of tradizionale goes a long way. In fact, its viscosity and intense flavor restrict its use. It is best sipped or frugally drizzled over food just before serving. Cooking with it is not recommended,

since heat tends to destroy its aromatic qualities.

For most culinary purposes, an artisan-style condimenti balsamic vinegar, made in the traditional method but aged for a shorter period, or a high-quality commercial vinegar, made from cooked grape must and aged wine vinegar, are a cook's best choice. With a few exceptions, the recipes in this book call for high-quality commercially produced vinegar or condimenti, although some recipies would undoubtedly benefit from the more expensive authentic tradizionale.

Since no two vinegars taste the same, it is important to sample each one before using it. Some vinegars will have a mellow, round, woody taste with a concentrated fruity start and an acidic end. Younger ones will have a more assertive acidic note that need to be balanced by another component. In any case, the vinegar should have both sweet and sour notes that balance harmoniously. It is best to store all types of balsamic vinegar in a cool, dark place.

Many of the recipes in this book were inspired by classic Italian dishes or use balsamic vinegar in traditional ways and flavor combinations. Others use the wonderfully complex, deep, earthy notes of balsamic vinegar as a jumping-off point. A splash is usually enough to give any dish an extraordinary depth.

STARTERS

*T*raditionally, aceto balsamico *is used sparingly as a condiment or seasoning. Added to a marinade to tenderize and flavor foods, stirred into a dish at the end of cooking, or simply drizzled on top of a cooked dish from a cruet set at the table, balsamic vinegar can add sparkle to an array of starters. Soups get a lift with some vinegar stirred in at the last moment, as in the Minestrone Modena-Style. Tuna Carpaccio gets its soulful note from a squiggle of mayonnaise flavored with balsamic. Parmesan-Crusted Asparagus is splashed with balsamic vinegar just before serving.*

The Italian antipasti table, or appetizer spread, is a perfect opportunity to present an array of dishes that more fully incorporate balsamic vinegar. Italian cooks often serve fresh vegetables, raw or cooked, with nothing more than a shallow bowl of fine aceto balsamico as a dipping sauce and a little coarse salt for seasoning. For a heartier appetizer, set out a mélange of brightly colored fresh vegetables on a beautiful ceramic platter with several small bowls of variously flavored and textured dipping sauces.

Vegetables a scapece, *that is, marinated in vinegar, are an indispensable element of the antipasti table and illustrate another of balsamic vinegar's virtues. In this chapter, grilled zucchini, pan-roasted bell peppers, and caponata (oven-roasted eggplant and tomatoes) are all enlivened by standing or cooking in a balsamic marinade or sauce.*

Choose from one of the soups and appetizers that follow for a tantalizing opening course, or mix and match several of the starters, side dishes, and salads and create a vegetable buffet complex and satisfying enough for an entire meal.

ITALIAN GAZPACHO

※◆※

*A few carefully chosen additions to the traditional Spanish gazpacho give the cold tomato
and vegetable soup a distinctly Italian flair. Serve it with crusty bread or sprinkle with croutons.
Note that this soup must be refrigerated for at least four hours. (photograph on page 21)*

SERVES 6 TO 8

*3 large ripe tomatoes (approximately 1 1/2 pounds),
    seeded and cut into 2-inch pieces*

*1 large cucumber (approximately 12 ounces), peeled, halved length-
    wise, seeded, and sliced into 1/2-inch-thick half moons*

*1 yellow or red bell pepper, stemmed, seeded and cut
    into 1-inch pieces*

1 small red onion, coarsely chopped

1 large garlic clove, finely chopped

1 1/2 cups tomato juice

1/3 cup balsamic vinegar

1/2 teaspoon salt

1/4 teaspoon red pepper flakes

1/3 cup chopped basil leaves, for garnish

Extra virgin olive oil, for serving

In a food processor fitted with the metal blade, combine the tomatoes, cucumber, bell pepper, onion, and garlic. Pulse a few times until the vegetables are coarsely chopped. Add the tomato juice, vinegar, salt, and red pepper flakes and process until the vegetables are finely chopped. Do not overprocess; the gazpacho should not be smooth. If necessary, process the gazpacho in batches.

Transfer to a large bowl and cover tightly. Refrigerate until chilled, at least 4 hours or overnight. Adjust the seasoning to taste, if necessary, before serving.

To serve, ladle the cold soup into individual chilled soup bowls, then sprinkle with the chopped basil. Serve with a cruet of olive oil so guests can drizzle their soup with oil to taste.

MINESTRONE
MODENA-STYLE

·━·◆·━·

The northern Italian region and city of Modena, home of aceto balsamico tradizionale, *are also well known
for their pork dishes. This thick, hearty vegetable and bean soup gets its intensity from* pancetta,
*an unsmoked seasoned bacon available in Italian food stores. If necessary, substitute slab bacon—but first simmer
it in water to cover for 5 minutes, then drain, pat dry, and chop. Because the vinegar is stirred in at the end, use the
best brand you can find—the better the vinegar, the richer the flavor it will impart to the soup.*

SERVES 6 TO 8

1 tablespoon olive oil

4 ounces pancetta, cut into 1/4-inch dice

1 yellow onion, coarsely chopped

1 celery rib with leaves, cut into 1/4-inch-thick slices

1 carrot, cut into 1/4-inch-thick rounds

*2 zucchini, cut in half lengthwise and sliced into
    1/4-inch-thick half moons*

2 garlic cloves, finely chopped

2 firmly packed cups (6 ounces) shredded savoy cabbage

*1 pound ripe Roma tomatoes, peeled, seeded, and cut into
    1/2-inch cubes, or one 16-ounce can peeled tomatoes,
    chopped, with juices*

2 cups water

*1 3/4 cups homemade beef, chicken, or vegetable broth,
    or low-sodium canned broth*

1 cup dry red wine

1 teaspoon salt

1 teaspoon dried thyme

1/8 teaspoon ground cloves

1/4 teaspoon freshly ground black pepper

*One 19-ounce can cannellini (white kidney) beans,
    rinsed and drained*

3 tablespoons balsamic vinegar

In a large soup pot, heat the oil over medium heat. Add the pancetta and cook, stirring occasionally, until browned, approximately 5 minutes. Add the following ingredients in order, cooking each for 1 minute before adding the next: onion, celery, carrot, zucchini, garlic, and cabbage.

Add the tomatoes and bring to a simmer over high heat. Stir in the water, broth, red wine, salt, thyme, cloves, and pepper. Bring to a boil. Reduce the heat to low and simmer until the vegetables are tender, approximately 1 hour. Stir in the beans and cook for 5 minutes, just until heated through. Stir in the balsamic vinegar. Serve hot.

Note: For a delicious vegetarian soup, omit the pancetta and use vegetable broth.

FRESH VEGETABLES
WITH ASSORTED DIPPING SAUCES

Seek out seasonal vegetables at their peak for this classic antipasto. Serve with two or more of the recipes listed below—found in the condiment and salad chapters—as dipping sauces. Or, for a delightfully simple appetizer, accompany the vegetables with a bowl of the finest balsamic vinegar available and a little coarse salt for seasoning.

SERVES 6 TO 8

Balsamic Mayonnaise (see page 45) mixed with chopped fresh chives or fresh basil

Roasted Garlic Conserve (see page 44)

Creamy Gorgonzola Dressing (see page 58)

Orange-Rosemary Vinaigrette (see page 60)

2 pounds assorted raw and blanched vegetables, in any combination, such as:

> *raw celery sticks; carrot sticks or baby carrots; green onions, trimmed; fennel, thinly sliced; cherry tomatoes; red or yellow bell peppers, stemmed, seeded, and cut into 1/2-inch-wide strips*

Blanched broccoli florets, cauliflower florets, baby artichokes, asparagus spears, small new potatoes, well-scrubbed and unpeeled

To blanche the vegetables, bring a large pot of salted water to a boil. In batches, cook the vegetables until al dente, approximately 4 minutes. Drain and rinse under cold water to stop the cooking.

On a large serving platter, place the dips in bowls and surround with the vegetables.

FRIED ARTICHOKES
IN SEMOLINA BATTER

❖❖❖

Instead of squeezing lemon juice over deep-fried foods, why not sprinkle them with a little balsamic vinegar as many Italians do? These golden-brown artichokes in a crunchy coating can be a cocktail snack, a warm first course, or even a side dish. Durum semolina flour is sometimes marketed as pasta flour.

SERVES 4 TO 6

1 large lemon, halved
6 medium artichokes (approximately 6 ounces each),
*   preferably with the stems still attached*
Vegetable oil for deep-frying
1/2 cup all-purpose flour
1/2 cup durum semolina flour
1/2 teaspoon salt, plus more to taste
1/4 teaspoon freshly ground black pepper
3 large eggs
Balsamic vinegar, for serving

Squeeze the lemon over a medium bowl, add the squeezed lemon halves to the juice, and fill the bowl halfway with cold water. Working with one artichoke at a time, snap off and discard the tough dark green leaves, revealing the light green cone of tender leaves. Using a sharp paring knife, cut off the cone where it meets the thick artichoke base. Trim away all of the dark green skin from the base and stem. Use the tip of the knife to cut out any purple leaves and the hairy choke from the center of the base; discard.

Cut the artichoke base lengthwise into 1/4-inch-thick slices. Place in the lemon water. Repeat with the remaining artichokes.

Preheat the oven to 200 degrees F. Line a baking sheet with paper towels. Pour oil into a large, heavy saucepan until it is half-full and heat to 360 degrees F. (An electric deep fryer works best.)

Drain the artichoke slices and pat dry with paper towels.

In a medium bowl, combine the flour, semolina, salt, and pepper. In another medium bowl, beat the eggs well. In batches, dip the artichoke slices in the egg, then coat with the flour mixture, shaking off excess flour. Place the coated artichoke slices on wire cake racks. In batches without crowding, deep-fry the artichoke slices until crisp and golden brown, about 4 minutes. With a large skimmer or slotted spoon, transfer to the paper towel–lined baking sheet and keep warm in the oven.

Season the artichokes with salt to taste. Serve immediately, passing a cruet of balsamic vinegar so guests can sprinkle on vinegar as they wish.

PARMESAN-CRUSTED ASPARAGUS
WITH BALSAMIC VINEGAR

❖

Balsamic vinegar is often sprinkled over thin wedges of Parmigiano-Reggiano, another of Emilia-Romagna's prized delicacies, or served as a dip for cooked asparagus. This warm appetizer combines both ideas—baked spears of asparagus get an ivory topping of shaved cheese. Indulge yourself with the finest balsamico you can find.

SERVES 4

*40 thin spears asparagus (approximately 1 pound),
    tough stems snapped off and discarded*
1 tablespoon extra virgin olive oil
*1 ounce Parmesan cheese curls (shaved off a large chunk
    of cheese with a vegetable peeler)*
Freshly ground black pepper, to taste
Balsamic vinegar, for serving

Preheat the oven to 450 degrees F. Place the asparagus in a single layer on a nonstick baking sheet. Drizzle with the olive oil and toss well, coating the asparagus completely. Spread the Parmesan curls over the top half of the asparagus spears.

Bake in the top one-third of the oven until the cheese is melted and the asparagus is barely tender, 12 to 15 minutes. Season with pepper to taste.

Using a metal spatula, transfer the asparagus to warm plates. Serve immediately with a cruet of balsamic vinegar, allowing guests to sprinkle their asparagus with vinegar to taste.

ROASTED CAPONATA
ON BRUSCHETTA

❖❖❖❖

Caponata, a Sicilian sweet-and-sour vegetable relish, is usually simmered for a long time. Here, however, the vegetables'
natural sugars are brought out by a light roasting in the oven. Heaped on slices of grilled bread, this is a flavorful,
but light, antipasto. For best results, make this at the height of tomato season, when tomatoes are bursting with flavor.

SERVES 4 TO 6

Roasted Caponata:

1 large eggplant (1 1/4 pounds), cut into 1-inch cubes

2 1/2 teaspoons salt

1 yellow onion, cut into 1/2-inch dice

1 red bell pepper, cut into 1/2-inch squares

1 celery rib, cut into 1/4-inch-thick slices

1 carrot, cut into 1/4-inch-thick rounds

4 tablespoons olive oil

1/4 teaspoon red pepper flakes

2 large garlic cloves, finely chopped

1 pound ripe Roma tomatoes, peeled, seeded, and chopped, or
*   one 16-ounce can peeled tomatoes, chopped, with juices*

1 teaspoon dried oregano

1/2 cup brine-cured olives, pitted and coarsely chopped

3 tablespoons small capers, preferably preserved in balsamic
*   vinegar (available in specialty stores)*

2 tablespoons sugar

2 tablespoons balsamic vinegar

1 loaf Italian bread, cut into 16 slices approximately 1/2 inch thick

2 tablespoons extra virgin olive oil, for brushing

To make the caponata, place the eggplant in a colander and toss with 1 1/2 teaspoons of the salt. Let stand to release some of its bitter juices, approximately 1 hour. Rinse well under cold running water, then pat dry with paper towels.

Preheat the oven to 450 degrees F. In a large roasting pan, toss the eggplant, onion, bell pepper, celery, and carrot with 2 tablespoons of the oil, the remaining 1 teaspoon salt, and the red pepper flakes. Bake in the top one-third of the oven, stirring occasionally, until the vegetables are tender and lightly browned around the edges, approximately 1 hour.

Meanwhile, in a medium saucepan, heat the remaining 2 tablespoons oil over medium heat. Add the garlic and cook for 2 minutes until golden. Add the tomatoes and oregano, and bring to a simmer. Cook, uncovered, until thickened, approximately 20 minutes. Stir in the olives, capers, and sugar and cook for 5 minutes. Stir in the balsamic vinegar.

In a medium bowl, combine the roasted vegetables with the tomato sauce. Let cool to room temperature. Cover tightly with plastic wrap and refrigerate until ready to serve, up to 3 days. Let the caponata stand at room temperature for 1 hour before serving. Adjust the seasoning if necessary.

Prepare a fire in a kettle-type charcoal grill. When the hot coals turn white, spread them evenly in the bottom of the grill. Grill the bread slices on one side only for 1 to 2 minutes, until toasted. Or, toast the bread slices in a preheated broiler with the rack positioned 4 inches from the source of heat. Brush the toasted sides with the olive oil.

To serve, arrange the bread slices toasted side up on a serving platter and spoon the caponata onto them.

GRILLED ZUCCHINI
IN MINT-BALSAMIC MARINADE

Zucchine a scapece (zucchini marinated in vinegar) is a classic antipasto. The zucchini are often simmered or fried, but the smoky flavor imparted by grilling complements the caramel notes found in balsamic vinegar. Start this dish at least 6 hours ahead of serving to allow for marinating.

SERVES 4 TO 6

8 zucchini (approximately 2 pounds), cut diagonally into 1/2-inch-wide strips

1/3 cup plus 2 tablespoons extra virgin olive oil

2 tablespoons balsamic vinegar

1 tablespoon red wine vinegar

1 garlic clove, crushed through a press

1/4 teaspoon salt

1/4 teaspoon freshly ground black pepper

1 tablespoon chopped fresh mint leaves

Prepare a fire in a kettle-type charcoal grill. When the hot coals turn white, spread them evenly in the bottom of the grill. In a large bowl, toss the zucchini with the 2 tablespoons olive oil. Grill the zucchini, turning once, until just tender, approximately 5 minutes. Transfer to a serving platter.

In a medium bowl, whisk together the balsamic vinegar, wine vinegar, garlic, salt, and pepper. Gradually whisk in the remaining 1/3 cup of olive oil. Pour over the zucchini and let stand until the zucchini are cool. Cover tightly with plastic wrap and let stand at room temperature for at least 4 hours. Serve at room temperature. (The zucchini can be prepared up to 3 days ahead, covered and refrigerated. Remove from the refrigerator 1 hour before serving.)

TUNA CARPACCIO
WITH BALSAMIC MAYONNAISE

❖❖❖

Harry's Bar in Venice popularized beef carpaccio, thinly sliced raw beef splashed with a pale mayonnaise-like dressing. The dish was named for the painter Vittore Carpaccio, whose canvases often featured a strong red palette with accents of white. This updated version uses fresh tuna instead of beef. Buy a large piece of the best tuna available (Japanese fish stores will probably carry a "sushi grade" tuna), and slice the fish at home—or ask the fish store to do it for you.

SERVES 4

1-pound piece of skinless, best-quality, very fresh tuna,
*   preferably from the center section*

1/2 cup Balsamic Mayonnaise (see page 45)

1 tablespoon balsamic vinegar

1 bunch fresh arugula (approximately 6 ounces), tough stems
*   discarded, well rinsed, and patted dry*

4 teaspoons coarsely chopped capers, preferably preserved
*   in balsamic vinegar (available in specialty stores)*

1 tablespoon snipped fresh chives

Using a very sharp, long, thin-bladed carving knife, cut the fish crosswise against the grain into 16 thin (approximately 1/8- to 1/4-inch-thick) slices, firmly pressing down on the fish, and cutting off the slices just below where you are pressing.

In a small bowl, thin the mayonnaise with the vinegar. Transfer to a small plastic storage bag. Squeeze the mayonnaise into one corner of the bag. With scissors, snip off the corner of the bag to make a small opening. Set aside carefully.

Divide the arugula among four chilled dinner plates. Arrange one-fourth of the tuna slices in overlapping fans on each plate. Squeeze the mayonnaise over the tuna and arugula in long, thin strokes and squiggles. Sprinkle each serving with capers and chives and serve immediately.

PAN-ROASTED PEPPERS WITH GOAT CHEESE
ON FRIED POLENTA SQUARES

❖

Roasted red bell peppers are tasty, but peeling them can be a bother. This recipe makes melt-in-your-mouth peppers in an easy pan-roasted method that gets a sweet-and-sour tang from balsamic vinegar and a little sugar. These peppers are also delicious as a side dish—pair them with grilled sausages. (photograph on page 20)

SERVES 6

Polenta Squares:

2 cups water

1 teaspoon salt

1 cup yellow cornmeal, preferably stone-ground

1 cup milk

3 tablespoons olive oil

*3 red bell peppers, stemmed, seeded, and cut into
1/3-inch-thick strips*

*3 yellow bell peppers, stemmed, seeded, and cut into
1/3-inch-thick strips*

2 large garlic cloves, thinly sliced

5 tablespoons balsamic vinegar

3/4 teaspoon salt

1/4 teaspoon freshly ground black pepper

1 1/2 teaspoons sugar

Olive oil, for greasing

4 ounces goat cheese, crumbled

To make the polenta, pour 2 cups of water and the salt into the heatproof top part of a double boiler and bring to a boil directly over high heat. (If the top part is glass or not heatproof, use a metal bowl set over a saucepan of boiling water.) Bring 2 inches of water to a boil in the bottom part of the double boiler and insert the top part.

In a medium bowl, mix the cornmeal with the milk until smooth. Whisk into the salted water until smooth and con-

tinue whisking until the polenta thickens, approximately 1 minute. Cook over medium heat, whisking occasionally, until the polenta is very thick, 25 to 30 minutes. Add water to the bottom part of the double boiler as needed.

Pour the polenta into a lightly oiled 8- by 4- by 3-inch loaf pan and smooth the top. Press plastic wrap directly on the top of the polenta (to prevent a skin from forming) and poke a few slits in the wrap to allow the steam to escape. Let cool to room temperature. Refrigerate until chilled, at least 1 hour or overnight.

To make the peppers, in a large skillet, heat the oil over medium low heat. Add the peppers, garlic, 3 tablespoons of vinegar, salt, and pepper. Cover and simmer, stirring occasionally, until tender, 25 to 30 minutes. Stir in the remaining vinegar and the sugar. Increase the heat to medium high and cook, stirring often, until the liquid has reduced and the peppers are glazed, approximately 2 minutes. Keep the peppers warm. (The peppers can be prepared up to 3 days ahead, covered and refrigerated.)

Heat a griddle or two large skillets until hot, then wipe well with a paper towel dipped in olive oil. Unmold the polenta and cut into 12 slices. Cook the slices on the griddle, turning once, until golden brown, approximately 6 minutes total.

To serve, place 2 polenta pieces on each warmed plate, top with the warm peppers, and sprinkle with the goat cheese.

SIDE DISHES AND CONDIMENTS

Balsamic vinegar, with its complex layers, is a condiment that can complement or act as a foil to the rich flavors of other dishes. Taking this role one step further, balsamic vinegar can also be incorporated into other accompaniments. I contorni, *meaning literally "that which surrounds," are the vegetable side dishes of Italian cuisine. In this chapter, vegetable side dishes are presented alongside condiments infused with balsamic vinegar, since they both offer robust flavors that complement the main course.*

Depending on its age and quality, balsamic vinegar can be used during the cooking process itself or added at the last moment. Young, mid-quality brands with a fair amount of acidity can replace regular red wine or cider vinegar in classic condiments such as chutneys, mustards, mayonnaise, and ketchup. Stocking the pantry with these balsamic-spiked condiments will help you add the flavors of balsamic vinegar to your favorite foods throughout the year. However, never cook with large amounts of tradizionale or well-aged balsamico. Not only is it far too precious, but also, the older the balsamico, the sweeter it becomes, and the more it loses the acidic bite that is so essential to balancing a dish. Vinegars with a syrupy consistency are better employed at the end of the cooking process to create a glaze, as in the Garlicky Roasted New Potatoes with Balsamic Vinegar or the Maple-Glazed Balsamic Carrots.

GRILLED RED ONIONS

❖❖❖❖❖

Tender, slightly sweet ribbons of grilled onion are a perfect accent for steaks and chops.
Choose a single herb or a combination that best complements the main course.

SERVES 4

1/4 cup balsamic vinegar

1 tablespoon chopped fresh sage, thyme, rosemary, or savory

1 teaspoon sugar

1/2 teaspoon salt

1/4 teaspoon freshly ground black pepper

1/4 cup extra virgin olive oil

4 red onions, cut into 1/2-inch-thick rounds

Olive oil, for brushing aluminum foil

In a small bowl, whisk together the vinegar, herbs, sugar, salt, and pepper. Gradually whisk in the oil.

Lightly brush four 12-inch squares of aluminum foil with oil. Overlap the slices of 1 onion on each foil square, and drizzle each with one-fourth of the vinegar mixture. Fold the foil into a tightly wrapped packet. (The onions can be prepared to this point up to 4 hours ahead and stored at room temperature.)

Prepare a fire in a kettle-type charcoal grill. When the hot coals turn white, spread them evenly in the bottom of the grill. Grill the onions in their foil packets, turning often, until the onions are tender and golden, 20 to 30 minutes. (Open a packet to check for doneness.) Open up the top of each foil packet to expose the onions and continue cooking until the liquid is almost evaporated, 5 to 7 minutes. Serve hot or at room temperature.

Note: The coals will burn down during cooking the onions, and may be too cool for grilling steaks or burgers, which cook best over high heat. When the onions are done, remove them from the grill, overwrap in another foil square, and set aside. Add fresh charcoal to the grill and wait until it is hot and turns white. Then cook the meat, returning the foil-wrapped onions to the grill during the last 5 minutes of cooking time to heat through.

Maple-Glazed Balsamic Carrots

Glazed carrots are a favorite side dish at family meals. This very easy version is an elegant makeover, resulting in al dente carrots with a sweet, piquant glaze. If you like softer, candied-style carrots, cook the covered carrots for an additional 2 minutes. Peeled baby carrots are available at most supermarkets, but you can also use regular carrots cut into sticks 1 1/2 inches long by 1/2 inch wide.

SERVES 4 TO 6

1 pound baby carrots

1/2 cup homemade beef broth or low-sodium canned broth
(or substitute chicken broth or fruit juice)

1/4 cup maple syrup

2 tablespoons unsalted butter

1/8 teaspoon salt

1/8 teaspoon freshly ground black pepper

2 tablespoons balsamic vinegar

In a medium skillet, combine the carrots, broth, maple syrup, butter, salt, and pepper. Bring to a boil over medium-high heat. Cover and cook for 3 minutes (or 5 minutes for softer, candied-style carrots). Increase the heat to high and uncover. Cook, stirring often, until the carrots are just tender and the liquid is reduced to 2 tablespoons, 5 to 6 minutes. Stir in the vinegar and cook until the liquid is reduced to a glaze, 1 to 2 minutes. Serve hot. (The carrots can be prepared up to 1 day ahead, covered, and refrigerated. Reheat the carrots, covered, in a skillet over low heat before serving.)

BRAISED BROCCOLI RAPE
WITH PROSCIUTTO AND PINE NUTS

Broccoli rape, or raab, which resembles broccoli but has more leaves and blossoms and thinner stems, is a staple in Italian kitchens during the cooler months. Its assertively bitter flavor is somewhat tamed by long cooking, although its strength is part of its charm. Serve broccoli rape as a side dish with sausages or smoked pork chops, or even toss it with cooked ziti to make a main course. (photograph on page 35)

SERVES 4

1/4 cup pine nuts

1 bunch broccoli rape (approximately 1 1/2 pounds)

1 tablespoon olive oil

2 ounces prosciutto, cut into 1/4-inch dice (approximately 1/2 cup)

2 large garlic cloves, crushed

1/3 cup homemade beef broth or low-sodium canned broth

1/4 teaspoon salt

1/4 teaspoon red pepper flakes

2 tablespoons balsamic vinegar

Heat a small skillet over medium heat. Add the pine nuts and cook, stirring almost constantly, until toasted, approximately 3 minutes. Transfer to a plate and set aside.

Cut the broccoli rape stems crosswise into 1/2-inch-thick pieces. Coarsely chop the leafy tops. Submerge the stems and tops, in a large bowl of cold water and agitate to loosen any grit. Drain, but do not shake off excess water.

In a large pot, heat the oil over medium heat. Add the prosciutto and garlic and cook until the garlic begins to brown slightly, approximately 2 minutes. Add the broccoli rape, broth, salt, and red pepper flakes. Cover and reduce the heat to medium-low. Cook until the broccoli rape is very tender, approximately 45 minutes. Stir in the vinegar and cook for 1 minute. Stir in the pine nuts. Serve hot. (The broccoli rape can also be prepared up to 1 day ahead, covered, and refrigerated. Reheat before serving).

SWEET-AND-SOUR RED CABBAGE
WITH PEARS AND CURRANTS

❖❖❖

This sweet-and-sour cabbage dish, from the Friuli region, shares its culinary heritage more closely with Switzerland and Germany than with Italy. It is a great make-ahead vegetable dish that gets better with reheating. The sweet notes in the balsamic vinegar harmonize with the other naturally sweet ingredients in the dish —onions, carrots, pears, and currants— to make this an out-of-the-ordinary braised cabbage. Serve it with roast quail or pheasant, grilled venison steaks, or sautéed pork chops. (photograph on page 34)

SERVES 6

2 tablespoons unsalted butter

1 onion, cut into 1/2-inch dice

2 carrots, cut into 1/2-inch dice

2 Bosc or Asian pears, peeled, cored, and cut into 1/2-inch dice

1 head red cabbage (approximately 2 pounds),
    cored and thinly sliced

1 cup canned pear nectar or fresh pear juice

1/3 cup dry red wine

1/3 cup dried currants

1/4 cup balsamic vinegar

1/4 cup firmly packed light brown sugar

1/2 teaspoon dried thyme

1 teaspoon salt

1/4 teaspoon freshly ground black pepper

In a large saucepan, heat the butter over medium heat. Add the onion and carrot and cover. Cook until the vegetables soften, approximately 5 minutes. Uncover and add the pears. Cook, uncovered, until the onion is golden brown, approximately 3 minutes.

Add the remaining ingredients and bring to a boil. Reduce the heat to medium-low and cover. Cook, stirring often, until the cabbage is tender, 50 minutes to 1 hour. Increase the heat to medium-high and cook, stirring often, until the liquid is evaporated, 5 to 7 minutes. Serve hot. (The cabbage can be prepared up to 3 days ahead, covered, and refrigerated. Reheat gently before serving.)

GARLICKY ROASTED NEW POTATOES
WITH BALSAMIC VINEGAR

❖

Humble roasted potatoes get a boost from a splash of balsamic vinegar. Use waxy, red-skinned, or Yukon Gold potatoes for best results. When onions, which give off liquid, are omitted from this standard side dish, the potatoes end up with a crispy brown exterior.

SERVES 6 TO 8

1/2 cup extra virgin olive oil

4 garlic cloves, crushed

Three 3-inch springs fresh rosemary or 1 1/2 teaspoons dried rosemary

9 medium red-skinned or Yukon Gold potatoes (approximately 2 1/2 pounds), cut into 1-inch chunks

1 teaspoon salt

1/4 teaspoon freshly ground black pepper

2 tablespoons balsamic vinegar

In a small saucepan over low heat, cook the oil and garlic until the garlic begins to color. Do not brown the garlic. Remove from heat and add the rosemary. Cover and let steep for 30 minutes.

Preheat the oven to 400 degrees F. Strain the oil into a roasting pan large enough to hold the potatoes in one layer. Add the potatoes, salt, and pepper and toss well to coat the potatoes completely. Bake in the top one-third of the oven, scraping up and turning the potatoes occasionally with a metal spatula, until the potatoes are crispy and tender, approximately 50 minutes. Sprinkle with the vinegar and toss; bake 5 minutes longer. Serve immediately.

ROASTED GARLIC CONSERVE

❖

Spread this onto bread, spoon it next to grilled lamb chops, slather it over a hamburger, or turn it into a salad dressing (see page 61)—you'll find plenty of uses for this zesty condiment.

MAKES 3/4 CUP

3 large, plump heads garlic (approximately 9 ounces)

4 tablespoons extra virgin olive oil

3 anchovy fillets in oil, drained

1/4 teaspoon salt

1 tablespoon balsamic vinegar

1 1/2 teaspoons chopped fresh rosemary or 3/4 teaspoon dried rosemary

1/4 teaspoon freshly ground black pepper

Preheat the oven to 325 degrees F. Cut each garlic head in half horizontally, keeping the cloves intact in their cluster. Do not remove the husk surrounding each head. Place the halves side by side on a large piece of aluminum foil and drizzle with 1 tablespoon of the oil. Tightly wrap the garlic in the foil and place on a baking sheet. Bake until the garlic is tender, 30 to 40 minutes. Set aside until cool enough to handle. Squeeze the cooked garlic out of the hulls into a small bowl. Discard the hulls and husk.

On a work surface, sprinkle the anchovies with the salt. Chop and smear the anchovies to form a paste and scrape into the bowl with the garlic. Mix in the vinegar, rosemary, and pepper. Gradually stir in the remaining 3 tablespoons of oil. (The conserve can be prepared up to 3 days ahead, tightly covered, and refrigerated.)

SPICY BLUEBERRY CHUTNEY

❖

Keep a jar of this versatile, chunky chutney in the refrigerator to serve with grilled chicken or pork chops or curried dishes.

MAKES 2 CUPS

2 cups blueberries, fresh or frozen

1 cup golden raisins

3/4 cup firmly packed light brown sugar

1/2 cup balsamic vinegar

1/2 cup finely chopped crystallized ginger

1/3 cup finely chopped onion

1 jalapeño, seeded and finely chopped

1 garlic clove, crushed through a press

Grated zest of 1 large lemon

1 cinnamon stick

1/8 teaspoon ground mace

1/8 teaspoon ground cloves

Combine all of the ingredients in a medium, heavy-bottomed, nonreactive saucepan. Bring to a boil over high heat, stirring often to avoid scorching. Reduce the heat to low and simmer, stirring occasionally, until very thick, 15 to 20 minutes. Cool completely. (The chutney can be prepared up to 1 week ahead, covered tightly, and refrigerated. For storage of up to 3 months, transfer the hot chutney to sterilized canning jars, cool completely, and store in the refrigerator.)

SWEET-ONION MARMALADE

❖◆❖

*Not too sweet, this condiment complements
grilled meats, chicken, and salmon, and is terrific
as a topping for pizza or bagels.*

MAKES 2 CUPS

1 tablespoon unsalted butter

1 tablespoon vegetable oil

*3 red onions (approximately 1 1/2 pounds), sliced into
1/4-inch-thick half moons*

1/2 cup dry red vermouth or dry red wine

1/4 cup firmly packed light brown sugar

1/2 teaspoon salt

1/4 teaspoon freshly ground black pepper

1/4 cup balsamic vinegar

*1 tablespoon chopped fresh rosemary or 1 1/2 teaspoons
dried rosemary*

1 tablespoon chopped fresh thyme or 1 1/2 teaspoons dried thyme

In a medium, heavy-bottomed, nonreactive saucepan, heat
the butter and oil over medium heat. Add the onions and
cover. Cook, stirring occasionally, until softened, approximately 5 minutes. Add the vermouth, brown sugar, salt, and
pepper and bring to a boil. (If using dried herbs, add them
now.) Reduce the heat to medium-low and cover. Simmer
until the onions are very tender, approximately 40 minutes.

Add the vinegar, rosemary, and thyme. Increase the heat to
high and cook, uncovered, stirring often, until the liquid
is reduced to a glaze, 3 to 5 minutes. Let cool to room temperature before serving. (The marmalade can be prepared
up to 1 week ahead, covered, and refrigerated. Bring to
room temperature before serving.)

BALSAMIC MAYONNAISE

❖◆❖

*This is a splendid condiment, ready to add a touch of
class to the most humble sandwiches and salads. You may
substitute 1/4 cup liquid egg substitute (at room
temperature) for the raw egg, if you wish. For an herbed
variation, stir 1/3 cup of finely chopped fresh basil into
the finished mayonnaise. (photograph on page 46)*

MAKES APPROXIMATELY 1 1/2 CUPS

1 large egg, at room temperature

2 tablespoons balsamic vinegar

1 tablespoon Dijon mustard

3/4 teaspoon salt

1/8 teaspoon freshly ground white pepper

3/4 cup vegetable oil

1/2 cup olive oil

In a blender, process the egg, 1 tablespoon of the balsamic
vinegar, mustard, salt, and pepper. With the blender running, slowly pour in the vegetable oil, one drop at a time,
until the mixture has become creamy; once creamy, add the
oil (first the remaining vegetable oil and then the olive oil)
in a thin, steady stream. It is critical not to add oil too
quickly or the mayonnaise will not emulsify. Use a rubber
spatula to scrape down the inside of the blender to ensure
that all the ingredients are thoroughly combined. Transfer
the mayonnaise to a bowl and stir in the remaining 1 tablespoon balsamic vinegar. Cover tightly with plastic wrap
and refrigerate until ready to use. (The mayonnaise can be
prepared up to 3 days ahead, covered, and refrigerated.)

APPLE CIDER AND BALSAMIC VINEGAR MUSTARD

❖

Mustard is traditionally made from wine, wine or fruit vinegar, or, less commonly, verjuice. Here, a combination of balsamic vinegar and apple cider is used. The mustard will need about a week to mellow. Your reward will be a spicy coarse mustard that will add zest to whatever it accompanies.

MAKES APPROXIMATELY 1 1/2 CUPS

7 tablespoons yellow mustard seeds

2 tablespoons black mustard seeds

2 tablespoons dried mustard powder, preferably Colman's

1/2 cup apple cider

1/2 cup balsamic vinegar

2 tablespoons honey

1 tablespoon minced shallot

1 large garlic clove, crushed

2 teaspoons salt

In a blender, grind the yellow and black mustard seeds and dried mustard until most of the seeds are almost ground to a powder, approximately 1 minute. You may need to stop the machine and scrape the pulverized seeds from the blades to avoid clogging. Transfer to a medium non-reactive bowl and stir in the cider. Let stand, uncovered, stirring occasionally, for 3 to 4 hours. (This allows the mustard to "breathe," giving it a more rounded flavor.)

Return to the blender and add the vinegar, honey, shallot, garlic, and salt. Blend until thick, approximately 1 minute. Transfer to a container, cover tightly, and refrigerate. Let mellow for 1 week before serving. (The mustard can be stored, covered and refrigerated, for up to 1 month.)

BALSAMIC TOMATO KETCHUP

❖

This homemade ketchup bears little resemblance to the bottled variety — with balsamic vinegar to add character, this is a highbrow version, destined for your best hamburgers. Note that it must be refrigerated for at least one day.

MAKES APPROXIMATELY 1 3/4 CUPS

2 pounds ripe Roma tomatoes, peeled, seeded, and finely chopped, or one 28-ounce can crushed tomatoes

1/4 cup balsamic vinegar

1/4 cup finely chopped onion (approximately 1/2 small onion)

1/4 cup finely chopped green bell pepper (1/4 medium bell pepper)

1 large garlic clove, crushed through a press

1 teaspoon celery salt

1/4 teaspoon freshly ground black pepper

1/8 teaspoon ground allspice

1/8 teaspoon ground cloves

1/8 teaspoon dried mustard powder

1/2 bay leaf

In a medium, heavy-bottomed saucepan, combine all the ingredients. Bring to a boil over medium heat, stirring often to avoid scorching. Reduce the heat to medium-low. Simmer uncovered, stirring often, until the ketchup is thick and reduces by half, 35 to 45 minutes. It will thicken more upon cooling. Let cool completely. Remove the bay leaf. If desired, process the ketchup in a blender or food processor until smooth. Transfer to a container, cover tightly, and refrigerate for at least 1 day before serving. (The ketchup can be prepared up to 2 weeks ahead, covered, and refrigerated. It will improve in flavor as it ages.)

SALADS AND VINAIGRETTES

*T*o most cooks, balsamic vinegar is most familiar and appreciated in salads and vinai-grettes. This chapter offers a variety of dressings, from light vinaigrettes to a creamy Gorgonzola, that can easily be adapted and used on your favorite green and vegetable salads. The distinctive smoky, woodsy flavor of balsamic vinegar is best paired with greens with pronounced flavors, such as spinach, chard, and bitter greens, or with earthy vegetables and legumes such as beets, lentils, mushrooms, and potatoes.

Italians have traditionally mixed their beloved condiment into salad dressings. However, in Modena and Reggio nell' Emilia, it is never used straight to dress greens, but is always blended with a regular red wine vinegar. This make sense since the locals typically use aceto balsamico tradizionale, *which is so thick and sweet it hardly resembles vinegar at all. Now, however, with so many young artisanal and high-quality commercial blends available, there really is no need to use such expensive vinegar for vinaigrettes. Available for a fraction of the price of tradizionale, these other vinegars are ideal for dressings. Once you dress a salad with one of these, you'll never want to touch the cheap supermarket variety of vinegars again.*

The best advice for preparing vinaigrettes is to taste the vinegar first. Depending on its quality and age, you may need to add a pinch of sugar or lemon juice to attain the desired balance. If the vinegar is well-aged and overly sweet and thick, try mixing a splash of wine vinegar or lemon juice into the dressing. If it is a younger, sharper vinegar, with plenty of acid, you may not need to bolster it with anything at all. And because balsamic vinegar has such an assertive flavor, you can use much less oil on salads.

CLASSIC MIXED GREEN SALAD
WITH BALSAMIC VINAIGRETTE

———◆———

*Most cooks are on the lookout for a classic vinaigrette that they can turn into a "house dressing"
to use again and again. This one will be a contender. The characteristic balsamic flavor is underscored
with a little brown sugar, given a touch of acidity with red wine vinegar, and accented with mustard.*

SERVES 4 TO 6; MAKES 1 CUP VINAIGRETTE

Balsamic Vinaigrette:

2 tablespoons balsamic vinegar

1 tablespoon red wine vinegar

1 tablespoon Dijon mustard

1 teaspoon light brown sugar

1 garlic clove, crushed through a press (optional)

1/2 teaspoon salt

1/4 teaspoon freshly ground black pepper

3/4 cup extra virgin olive oil

1 small red onion, thinly sliced

*1 large head green, red leaf, or Romaine lettuce,
    rinsed, dried, and torn into bite-sized pieces*

1 large ripe beefsteak tomato, cut into eighths

1 seedless cucumber, unpeeled, thinly sliced

Salt and freshly ground black pepper, to taste

To make the vinaigrette, in a medium bowl whisk all the ingredients except the oil until mixed. Gradually whisk in the oil until smooth.

In a small bowl, cover the onion with iced water and let stand for 10 minutes. Drain well. (Soaking the onion removes its sharp bite.)

In a large bowl, place the lettuce, drained onion, tomato, and cucumber, and add the dressing a little at a time, tossing gently and thoroughly until all the vegetables are evenly coated. Season with additional salt and pepper to taste. Serve immediately on chilled salad plates.

WARM SPINACH AND PEAR SALAD
WITH PANCETTA AND SHALLOT VINAIGRETTE

⟡

Warm, wilted salads make excellent opening courses for winter meals. This dressing, made with pancetta (an unsmoked, seasoned bacon), shallots, garlic, and balsamic vinegar, is especially flavorful. Depending on the age and sharpness of the vinegar, you may not need to mix in the red wine vinegar. If you cannot find pancetta, substitute slab bacon that has been simmered in water to cover for 5 minutes, drained, and patted dry. (photograph on page 48)

SERVES 4;
MAKES APPROXIMATELY 1 1/4 CUPS VINAIGRETTE

Pancetta and Shallot Vinaigrette:

8 slices pancetta (approximately 3 ounces)

3 tablespoons finely chopped shallots

1 garlic clove, finely chopped

3/4 cup olive oil

2 tablespoons balsamic vinegar

2 tablespoons red wine vinegar

2 teaspoons light brown sugar

1/2 teaspoon salt

1/4 teaspoon freshly ground black pepper

2 bunches fresh spinach (approximately 18 ounces), tough stems discarded, well-rinsed, and dried

2 ripe Comice or Bartlett pears, peeled, cored, and cut into thin wedges

In a large skillet, cook the pancetta over medium heat, turning once, until crisp and brown, approximately 5 minutes. Transfer to paper towels to drain. Pour off all but 2 tablespoons of fat from the skillet.

Add the shallots and garlic and cook, stirring, until they begin to brown slightly, approximately 1 minute. Add the oil, balsamic vinegar, wine vinegar, brown sugar, salt, and pepper and bring to a boil, whisking constantly. Remove from the heat.

In a large bowl, toss the spinach and pears, and add the dressing a little at a time, tossing gently and thoroughly, until the pears are evenly coated and the greens are wilted. Serve immediately, garnishing each salad with 2 pieces of pancetta.

MUSHROOM AND ARUGULA SALAD

WITH PARMESAN, CHIVES, AND BALSAMIC VINAIGRETTE

This is a refreshing first course for Mediterranean-style meals. Use fresh white button or
cremini mushrooms, since other mushrooms (such as shiitakes or wild mushrooms) are at their best when cooked.
Do not let the dressed mushrooms stand for more than a few minutes, or they will wilt.

SERVES 4 TO 6

1 pound white button or cremini mushrooms

Balsamic Vinaigrette (see page 52)

2 bunches arugula (approximately 4 ounces each),
    tough stems discarded, well-rinsed, and dried

Approximately 2 ounces Parmesan cheese curls (shaved
    from a large chunk of cheese with a vegetable peeler)

1/4 cup fresh snipped chives

Fill a large bowl with cold water and add the mushrooms. Agitate quickly and briefly to loosen any grit. Lift out the mushrooms and place in a colander to drain. Using a sharp knife or a food processor fitted with the thin slicing blade, thinly slice the mushrooms.

In a medium bowl, toss the mushrooms with the dressing until evenly coated. Arrange clusters of the arugula on chilled salad plates. Top with the mushrooms and then the Parmesan cheese curls. Sprinkle with the chives and serve immediately.

TOMATO, MOZZARELLA, AND BASIL SALAD
WITH SUN-DRIED TOMATO VINAIGRETTE

―◈―

This salad is on the menu of almost every Italian restaurant in the United States, but unfortunately is not always as delicious as it can be. It should be made with the ripest, most flavorful tomatoes, excellent mozzarella (preferably handmade from a cheese store or Italian grocer), and fresh basil. The dressing, thickened with puréed sun-dried tomatoes, underlines the fresh ones, making this salad a tomato lover's dream.

SERVES 6:
MAKES APPROXIMATELY 1 1/3 CUPS VINAIGRETTE

Sun-Dried Tomato Vinaigrette:

*1/3 cup firmly packed sun-dried tomatoes in oil,
    drained, oil reserved*

3 tablespoons balsamic vinegar

1 garlic clove, crushed

1/4 teaspoon salt

1/4 teaspoon red pepper flakes

2/3 cup extra virgin olive oil

3 tablespoons reserved sun-dried tomato oil

*2 bunches arugula (4 ounces each), tough stems discarded,
    well-rinsed, and dried*

*4 large ripe beefsteak tomatoes (8 ounces each),
    ends discarded, cut crosswise into 18 slices*

12 ounces fresh mozzarella, cut into 12 slices

*12 large basil leaves, rolled and cut into thin strips
    (approximately 1/2 cup)*

To make the vinaigrette, in a blender process all of the ingredients except the oils until combined. With the machine running, gradually pour in the olive oil and reserved sun-dried tomato oil until the vinaigrette is smooth.

On the top half of a chilled dinner plate, arrange one-sixth of the arugula in a bouquet. Below the arugula, overlap 3 slices of tomato and 2 slices of mozzarella in a fan. Spoon approximately 3 tablespoons of the dressing over the salad. Sprinkle with basil. Repeat with the remaining ingredients on five other chilled plates. Or, for a beautiful antipasto plate, arrange all the ingredients attractively on a serving platter. Serve immediately.

CABBAGE AND APPLE SLAW
WITH CREAMY GORGONZOLA DRESSING

‹—◆—◆—◆—›

*This rich and sophisticated coleslaw would go well with a holiday buffet. Italian Gorgonzola is
one of the premier blue cheeses, and makes a world-class, thick, creamy dressing. The dressing would also
be wonderful on crisp Romaine lettuce hearts. For best results, prepare the coleslaw at least 4 hours
ahead of time. For a pourable version, dilute it with a few tablespoons of milk, but do not dilute it for this slaw
— as it chills in the refrigerator, the cabbage juices will thin the dressing.*

SERVES 6 TO 8;
MAKES APPROXIMATELY 2 1/4 CUPS DRESSING

Creamy Gorgonzola Dressing:

3/4 cup Balsamic Mayonnaise (see page 45)
*   or prepared mayonnaise*

3/4 cup sour cream

1 tablespoon balsamic vinegar

1/2 teaspoon freshly ground black pepper

8 ounces sharp Gorgonzola cheese, crumbled

4 cups finely shredded green cabbage (approximately 12 ounces)

4 cups finely shredded red cabbage (approximately 12 ounces)

2 tart apples, such as Granny Smith, unpeeled, cored,
*   and chopped into 1/4-inch dice*

1/2 cup coarsely chopped walnuts

4 green onions, finely chopped

3 tablespoons balsamic vinegar, or to taste

Salt, to taste

1/4 teaspoon freshly ground black pepper

Chopped parsley, for garnish

To make the dressing, in a small bowl combine the
Balsamic Mayonnaise, sour cream, vinegar, and pepper.
Stir in the Gorgonzola.

In a large bowl, combine the green and red cabbage,
apples, walnuts, and green onions. Add the dressing and
vinegar and toss well. Cover and refrigerate until chilled,
at least 4 hours or overnight. Season with salt to taste, and
the pepper. Taste the coleslaw and season with additional
vinegar if necessary.

Serve chilled, sprinkled with the parsley.

ROASTED BEETS ON OAKLEAF LETTUCE
WITH ORANGE-ROSEMARY VINAIGRETTE

*Beets are making a comeback—and these delicious oven-roasted beets will help show you why.
Look for bunched beets with the greens still attached. If the greens are young, tender, and not bitter,
discard the tough stems, tear the greens into bite-sized pieces and substitute for some of the lettuce.
Note that the beets need to marinate for at least 2 hours. (photograph on page 49)*

SERVES 4 TO 6;
MAKES APPROXIMATELY 1 1/4 CUPS VINAIGRETTE

*3 beets (approximately 6 ounces each), red, golden,
or a combination, unpeeled and well-scrubbed*

Orange-Rosemary Vinaigrette:

1 large orange

2 tablespoons balsamic vinegar

1 tablespoon red wine vinegar

1 tablespoon minced shallot

1 tablespoon chopped fresh rosemary or 1 teaspoon dried rosemary

1 teaspoon light brown sugar

1/2 teaspoon salt

1/4 teaspoon freshly ground black pepper

3/4 cup extra virgin olive oil

*1 large head oakleaf lettuce, rinsed, dried,
and torn into bite-sized pieces*

Preheat the oven to 400 degrees F. Wrap each beet in aluminum foil and place on a baking sheet. Bake until the beets are tender, approximately 45 minutes. Let cool until easy enough to handle. Remove the foil, slip off the skins

and discard them. Cut the beets in half, and then into 1/2-inch-thick slices. Place in a bowl and set aside. If using different-colored beets, keep them in separate bowls or the colors will bleed.

To make the vinaigrette, grate the zest off the orange into a small bowl. (You should end up with 2 teaspoons of zest.) Using a serrated knife, cut away the rind and discard. Working over the bowl, cut out each section of orange from between the membranes and place the sections in the bowl. Squeeze the membranes to release the juices into the bowl, then discard the membranes.

In a blender, process the orange sections with the zest and juice, balsamic vinegar, red wine vinegar, shallot, rosemary, brown sugar, salt, and pepper. With the machine running, add the oil and blend until smooth and thickened. Pour half of the dressing over the beets and toss. Cover and refrigerate for at least 2 hours. Reserve the remaining dressing.

To serve, place the lettuce in a large bowl and add the dressing a little at a time and toss, gently and thoroughly, until the greens are lightly coated. Place the lettuce on chilled salad plates, then top with the beets. Serve chilled.

Lentil, Fennel, and Goat Cheese Salad
with Roasted Garlic Vinaigrette

❖

Crisp fennel, with its faint licorice flavor, combines with tender lentils to make a hearty salad for a buffet or picnic. It is better to make this dish ahead of time to allow the flavors to marry. If you are a fan of licorice flavors, chop the feathery fennel tops to sprinkle over the salad as a garnish—they have more kick than the bulb. Roasted Garlic Conserve (see page 44) is the basis for the heady dressing. This dish needs to marinate for at least 1 hour.

SERVES 8; MAKES APPROXIMATELY 1 CUP VINAIGRETTE

Roasted Garlic Vinaigrette:

1/4 cup Roasted Garlic Conserve (see page 44)

2 tablespoons balsamic vinegar

1 tablespoon red wine vinegar

1/4 teaspoon salt

1/8 teaspoon freshly ground black pepper

1/3 cup olive oil

8 cups water

2 cups dried lentils (approximately 1 pound), rinsed and sorted over

1 large onion, cut in half

2 garlic cloves, crushed

1/2 teaspoon salt, plus more to taste

1 cup finely chopped fennel bulb (approximately 1/2 medium head)

1 small red onion, finely chopped

1 carrot, finely chopped

1/3 cup chopped fresh celery

2 tablespoons balsamic vinegar

6 ounces goat cheese, crumbled

1/4 teaspoon freshly ground black pepper, or more to taste

Chopped fresh parsley or fennel tops, for garnish

To make the vinaigrette, in a medium bowl whisk all the ingredients but the oil together to mix. Gradually whisk in the oil until combined. Set the vinaigrette aside.

In a medium saucepan, combine the water, lentils, onion halves, and garlic. Bring to a boil over medium heat. Reduce the heat to low. Simmer uncovered for 15 minutes. Add the salt and continue cooking until the lentils are tender, 5 to 15 minutes, depending on the lentils. Drain and discard the onion and garlic.

In a large bowl, combine the lentils, fennel, red onion, carrot, celery, and vinegar. Toss with three-fourths of the vinaigrette and the goat cheese. Cover and refrigerate for at least 1 hour and up to 24 hours. Add the remaining vinaigrette and toss, then season with salt and pepper. Serve at room temperature, sprinkled with the chopped parsley or fennel tops.

YUKON GOLD POTATO AND PEA SALAD
WITH PESTO VINAIGRETTE

❖◆❖

Pesto is another Italian staple that benefits from the addition of balsamic vinegar.
Yukon Gold potatoes cook up especially firm with a yellow flesh, but any boiling potato will do. For
best results, prepare this salad at least 4 hours ahead of time to allow the flavors to develop.

SERVES 4 TO 6;
MAKES APPROXIMATELY 1 1/4 CUPS VINAIGRETTE

Pesto Vinaigrette:

1/2 cup freshly grated Parmesan cheese

1/4 cup firmly packed coarsely chopped fresh basil leaves

2 tablespoons balsamic vinegar

1 tablespoon red wine vinegar

1/2 teaspoon salt

1/4 teaspoon freshly ground black pepper

3/4 cup extra virgin olive oil

10 medium Yukon Gold or red-skinned potatoes
(approximately 2 pounds), unpeeled and well-scrubbed

2 celery ribs, cut into 1/8-inch-thick slices

1 cup thawed baby peas

1/4 teaspoon salt

1/4 teaspoon freshly ground black pepper

Basil leaves, for garnish

To make the vinaigrette, combine all of the ingredients except the oil in a blender. With the blender still running, gradually add the oil until the dressing is smooth.

Bring a large pot of lightly salted water to a boil over high heat. Add the potatoes and cook, uncovered, until the potatoes can be pierced with the tip of a sharp knife, approximately 20 minutes. Drain and rinse under cold water until cool enough to handle. Slice into 1/2-inch-thick rounds and place in a medium bowl.

Add the celery, peas, and three-fourths of the dressing. Cover and refrigerate for at least 4 hours or up to 1 day. Toss with the remaining dressing, salt, and pepper. Garnish with the basil leaves and serve chilled.

Main Courses

Balsamic vinegar, with its complex earthy and herbaceous layers, can add depth to a range of main courses. Depending on the age and character of the vinegar, it can be used as an ingredient or to finish a dish. A younger vinegar with lots of acid is ideal for marinades, tomato sauces, and meat and vegetable stews. An older, more viscous balsamic vinegar is best drizzled directly over grilled meats or poached fish before serving. In restaurants near Modena and Reggio nell' Emilia, waiters ceremoniously use eyedroppers to dispense ancient balsamico tradizionale onto meat courses at the table.

The main courses in this chapter illustrate the wide range of foods that balsamic vinegar complements. Its rich flavors can stand up to long-simmered cooking in dishes such as Sweet-and-Sour Lamb Shanks and Ziti with Pork, Olive, and Tomato Sauce. But it fares equally well with lighter meals such as Fettuccine with Green Beans, Potatoes, and Balsamic Pesto; Salmon with Gingered Balsamic Vinegar Sauce; and Swordfish and Red Bell Pepper Spiedini. In many of these dishes, the vinegar is used two ways—first in a marinade, then splashed over the top of the finished dish.

Adding balsamic vinegar after deglazing is one of the easiest and most satisfying ways to prepare a sauce. Whether you are cooking chicken, beef, or game, you can make the sauce in the pan the main course was cooked in. Simply raise the heat, add some more liquid to the pan juices, deglaze, reduce until the sauce thickens, and then stir in some vinegar and warm through. The flavor is unbeatable and clean up is a snap.

TOMATO AND MOZZARELLA PIZZA
WITH BALSAMIC PESTO

◆◆◆◆◆

Here's a home-style pizza that's easy to make. The dough is stretched and patted into a jelly roll pan, and topped with ripe tomatoes and cheese. After baking, the pizza is enhanced with a slathering of balsamic vinegar pesto.

SERVES 4 TO 6

Pizza Dough:

1 teaspoon active dry yeast

Pinch of sugar

1/4 cup warm water (100 to 110 degrees F.)

2 1/2 cups unbleached flour

1 teaspoon salt

3/4 cup cold water

2 tablespoons extra virgin olive oil, plus extra for brushing

Cornmeal, for sprinkling

Topping:

1/4 cup freshly grated Parmesan cheese

5 ripe Roma tomatoes, halved horizontally, squeezed gently to remove some of the seeds, and sliced into 1/4-inch-thick rounds

3/4 cup shredded mozzarella cheese, preferably handmade

1/4 cup Balsamic Pesto (see page 72)

To make the dough, in a small bowl sprinkle the yeast and sugar in the warm water. Let stand until creamy, approximately 5 minutes; stir to dissolve. Place the flour and salt in a food processor fitted with the metal blade and pulse to combine. In a liquid measuring cup, combine the yeast mixture, cold water, and oil. With the machine running, pour the liquids through the feed tube and process until the dough forms a ball. (If the dough is too wet, add flour, 1 tablespoon at a time, and process until a ball forms. If it

is dry and crumbly, add water, 1 tablespoon at a time.) Process the dough 45 seconds longer. Place the dough in a large plastic bag and close tightly. Let stand in a warm place until doubled in bulk (a finger inserted 1/2 inch into the dough will leave an impression), approximately 1 hour.

Preheat the oven to 450 degrees F. Sprinkle a thin layer of cornmeal over a 15- by 1-inch jelly roll pan. Pat and stretch the dough into the pan. Cover with plastic wrap and let stand until slightly puffy, approximately 15 minutes.

Sprinkle the dough with the Parmesan cheese. Arrange layers of the tomatoes over the dough, then sprinkle with the mozzarella. Bake in the top one-third of the oven until the underside of the crust is golden brown (lift with a metal spatula to check), 15 to 20 minutes. Spread the pizza with the pesto and let stand for 1 minute. To serve, cut into large rectangles. Serve hot.

Note: The dough can also be made by hand. Increase the warm water to 1 cup. (Eliminate the cold water, which is used to compensate for the friction-generated heat in a food processor.) In a small bowl, sprinkle the water with the yeast and sugar and let stand until creamy, approximately 5 minutes; stir to dissolve. Place the yeast mixture in a medium bowl and add the salt and oil. Gradually stir in enough of the flour to make a soft dough. Turn out onto a floured work surface and knead until dough is supple and elastic, approximately 10 minutes. Continue as above.

ZITI

WITH PORK, OLIVE, AND TOMATO SAUCE

❖—◆—❖

Natives of Emilia-Romagna often lace their tomato sauces with balsamic vinegar, which helps brighten
the flavors. Try to make this sauce 1 day, or up to 3 days ahead of serving, so it can mellow.

SERVES 6 TO 8;
MAKES APPROXIMATELY 5 1/2 CUPS SAUCE

Pork, Olive, and Tomato Sauce:

3 tablespoons olive oil

2 pounds meaty pork neck bones

1 yellow onion, chopped into 1/4-inch pieces

1 carrot, cut into 1/4-inch dice

1 celery rib, cut into 1/4-inch dice

2 garlic cloves, finely chopped

1 cup dry red wine

4 pounds ripe Roma tomatoes, peeled, seeded, and coarsely
*   chopped or two 28-ounce cans tomatoes, chopped, with juices*

1 tablespoon dried basil or 1/4 cup chopped fresh basil

2 teaspoons dried rosemary or 1 tablespoon chopped fresh rosemary

2 teaspoon dried oregano

1 teaspoon salt (less if using canned tomatoes)

1/2 teaspoon red pepper flakes, or to taste

1 bay leaf

1 cup black brine-cured olives, pitted and coarsely chopped

1/4 cup balsamic vinegar

1 1/2 pounds ziti or other dried tubular pasta, such as rigatoni
Freshly grated Parmesan cheese, for sprinkling on top

To make the sauce, in a large saucepan, heat 2 tablespoons
of the oil over medium-high heat. Add the pork, in batches
if necessary, and cook, turning occasionally, until browned,
approximately 8 minutes. Transfer to a plate.

Heat the remaining 1 tablespoon oil in the saucepan and
add the onion, carrot, and celery. Reduce the heat to medium and cover. Cook, stirring occasionally, until the vegetables soften, approximately 5 minutes. Uncover and cook
until the onions are golden brown, approximately 5 minutes.
Add the garlic and cook for 1 minute until lightly colored.
Add the red wine, increase the heat to high, and cook until
the wine reduces by half, approximately 3 minutes. Return
the pork to the pan and add the tomatoes with their juices.
Bring to a boil, skimming off any foam that rises to the
surface. Add the dried basil, rosemary, oregano, salt, red
pepper flakes, and bay leaf. If using fresh herbs, add them
to the sauce during the last 10 minutes of cooking.

Reduce the heat to low and cover partially. Simmer until
the meat is very tender and the sauce is thick, approximately
2 1/4 hours. Remove the pork and discard. (If desired,
remove the meat from the bones and stir the meat back
into the sauce.) Add the olives and balsamic vinegar and
cook until the olives are heated through. Skim off any fat
from the surface. (For best flavor, let cool to room temperature, cover, and refrigerate overnight.)

In a large pot bring 6 quarts of salted water to a boil. Add
the pasta and cook until barely tender, 8 to 10 minutes.
Drain well, then return to the pot. Add the pasta sauce
(reheat if necessary) and cook over low heat for 1 minute,
stirring constantly, so the pasta absorbs some sauce. Transfer
to a serving bowl. Serve immediately, with grated Parmesan.

FETTUCCINE WITH GREEN BEANS, POTATOES,
AND BALSAMIC PESTO

❖◆❖

Lynn Rosetto Kasper, in her seminal book on the cooking of Emilia-Romagna, The Splendid Table, *discusses how a little balsamic vinegar can invigorate basil pesto. In this hearty vegetarian main course, the pesto is tossed with fettuccine, green beans, and potatoes. Like all pestos, it can be used in many other dishes—spread it on pizza or mix it into potato salad. (photograph on page 65)*

SERVES 4 TO 6

Balsamic Pesto:

2 cups firmly packed fresh basil leaves
    (approximately 2 large bunches)
1/2 cup freshly grated Parmesan cheese
2 tablespoons pine nuts or coarsely chopped walnuts
1 garlic clove, crushed
1/2 teaspoon salt
1/8 teaspoon freshly ground black pepper
1/2 cup extra virgin olive oil
2 tablespoons balsamic vinegar

12 ounces green beans, trimmed, cut into 1-inch-long pieces
4 medium new potatoes (approximately 12 ounces), unpeeled,
    well-scrubbed, and cut into 1/2-inch cubes
1 pound dried fettuccine
Salt and freshly ground black pepper, to taste

To make the pesto, place the basil, cheese, pine nuts, garlic, salt, and pepper in a food processor fitted with the metal blade. (To make in a blender, pour 3 tablespoons of the olive oil into the bottom of the container before adding the other ingredients.) With the machine running, gradually add the oil; scrape down the sides as necessary, and process until smooth. Add the vinegar and pulse until combined. (The pesto can be prepared up to 3 days ahead, covered, and refrigerated. For storage of up to 3 weeks, smooth the top and pour on a 1/8-inch-thick layer of oil. To freeze for up to 3 months, make the pesto without the cheese. Before serving, thaw the pesto and stir in the cheese.)

Bring a medium saucepan of lightly salted water to a boil over high heat. Add the green beans and cook until al dente, approximately 4 minutes. Using a large skimmer, remove the green beans and transfer to a bowl of cold water. Keep the saucepan of water on the heat. Drain the green beans, place in a large bowl, and set aside. Add the potatoes to the boiling water and cook until tender, 10 to 15 minutes. Drain the potatoes and place in the bowl with the green beans.

Meanwhile, bring a large pot of lightly salted water to a boil over high heat. Add the fettuccine and cook, stirring often, until barely tender, 7 to 9 minutes. During the last minute of cooking, add the green beans and potatoes so they heat through. Drain, reserving approximately 1/2 cup of the cooking water. Return the pasta and vegetables to the still-warm pot. Add the pesto and toss, adding enough of the reserved cooking liquid to make a creamy sauce. Season with salt and pepper. Transfer to a heated serving bowl and serve family-style.

MEDITERRANEAN VEGETABLE STEW
WITH PARMESAN POLENTA

A big pot of this stew simmering on the stove top is a comforting treat, filling the house with savory aromas that forecast the flavors to come.

SERVES 8

Vegetable Stew:

1 eggplant (approximately 1 pound), unpeeled,
  cut into 1-inch pieces

2 zucchini (approximately 12 ounces), cut into 3/4-inch pieces

2 teaspoons salt

5 tablespoons olive oil

1 large red onion, cut into 1/4-inch pieces

2 celery ribs with leaves, cut into 1/4-inch-thick slices

1 red bell pepper, stemmed, seeded and cut into 3/4-inch squares

2 garlic cloves, finely chopped

1 cup dry red wine

One 28-ounce can peeled tomatoes, chopped, with juices,
  or 2 pounds ripe, fresh Roma tomatoes, peeled, seeded,
  and chopped

2 medium red-skinned potatoes (approximately 8 ounces),
  well-scrubbed, cut into 3/4-inch pieces

One 15-ounce can chick-peas, drained and rinsed

1/2 cup chopped fresh basil

3 tablespoons balsamic vinegar

Parmesan Polenta:

4 cups water

1 1/2 teaspoons salt

2 cups yellow cornmeal, preferably stone-ground

2 cups milk

1 1/2 cups freshly grated Parmesan cheese

To make the stew, place the eggplant and zucchini in a large colander and toss with 1 1/2 teaspoons of the salt. Let stand to release bitter juices, 30 minutes to 1 hour. Rinse well under cold running water, squeeze to remove the excess moisture, then pat dry with paper towels.

In a large, heavy-bottomed flameproof casserole or pot, heat 3 tablespoons of the oil over medium heat. Add the eggplant and zucchini and cook, stirring occasionally, until lightly browned, approximately 10 minutes. Transfer to a bowl and set aside.

Heat the remaining 2 tablespoons oil and add the onion, celery, and red pepper. Cover and cook until the onion is softened, approximately 5 minutes. Add the garlic and cook for 1 minute. Add the wine and increase the heat to high. Cook until the wine reduces by half, approximately 3 minutes. Stir in the tomatoes with their juices, and the potatoes. Bring to a boil, then reduce the heat to medium-low. Cook uncovered, stirring often, until the potatoes are tender, approximately 40 minutes. Stir in the chick-peas and basil and cook until the chick-peas are heated through, approximately 5 minutes. Stir in the vinegar.

Meanwhile, make the polenta, following the instructions found on page 33, stopping before the point when the polenta is poured into the loaf pan. When the polenta is done and very thick, whisk in the cheese. To serve, spoon the polenta into serving bowls and top with the vegetable stew. Serve hot.

POTATO AND CARAMELIZED ONION FRITTATA

WITH GORGONZOLA

❖

For a casual lunch, supper, or (of course) brunch, a frittata makes a satisfying entree. With a balsamic-spiked caramelized onion topping, this frittata is a little more complex than most, but worth the effort.

SERVES 6

Caramelized Onions:

2 tablespoons unsalted butter

*2 large yellow onions (approximately 1 1/4 pounds),
    cut into 1/8-inch-thick half moons*

1/4 teaspoon salt

1/8 teaspoon freshly ground black pepper

2 tablespoons balsamic vinegar

1 teaspoon sugar

*5 medium red-skinned potatoes (approximately 1 pound),
    unpeeled and well-scrubbed*

2 tablespoons olive oil

1 teaspoon salt

1/4 plus 1/8 teaspoon freshly ground black pepper

10 large eggs

*2 teaspoons chopped fresh rosemary or 3/4 teaspoon
    dried rosemary*

2 ounces sharp Gorgonzola, crumbled

To make the caramelized onions, in a medium nonstick skillet, melt the butter over medium heat. Add the onions, salt, and pepper. Cook, stirring often to avoid scorching, until the onions are very soft and deep golden brown, 12 to 15 minutes. Stir in the vinegar and sugar and cook until the vinegar is reduced to a glaze, about 1 minute. Keep the onions warm. (The onions can be prepared up to 3 days ahead, covered, and refrigerated. Reheat before using.)

Bring a large pot of salted water to a boil over high heat. Add the potatoes and cook for 10 minutes, until parboiled. Drain and rinse under cold water until cool enough to handle. Cut into 1/2-inch-thick slices, then chop coarsely.

In a 9- to 10-inch nonstick ovenproof skillet, heat the oil over medium heat. Add the potatoes, 1/2 teaspoon of the salt and 1/4 teaspoon of the pepper. Cook, uncovered, turning the potatoes occasionally, until they are browned and tender, 12 to 15 minutes. Spread the potatoes as evenly as possible in the skillet.

Position the broiler rack about 6 inches from the source of heat and preheat the broiler. In a medium bowl, whisk the eggs, rosemary, and the remaining 1/2 teaspoon salt and 1/8 teaspoon pepper until well combined. Pour over the potatoes and reduce the heat to medium-low. Using a rubber spatula, lift up the cooked part of the frittata, and tilt the skillet to allow the uncooked eggs to run underneath. Continue cooking, occasionally lifting the frittata and tilting the skillet as described, until the top is almost set, approximately 5 minutes. Sprinkle with the Gorgonzola. Broil until the frittata is puffed and the top is set, approximately 1 minute.

To serve, spread the top of the frittata with the warm onions and cut into wedges. Serve hot or warm.

SALMON
WITH GINGERED BALSAMIC VINEGAR SAUCE

⬥⬥◆⬥⬥

Grilled or broiled salmon is an elegant dish that can be put on the table in a hurry. Many Italians prefer to season their grilled fish with balsamico instead of the ubiquitous lemon wedge. This recipe gets an added East-West dimension from the vinegar's infusion with ginger, green onions, and garlic.

SERVES 4

1/4 cup balsamic vinegar

1 tablespoon shredded fresh ginger (use the coarse holes of a cheese grater)

1 tablespoon minced green onion

1 garlic clove, crushed through a press

Nonstick vegetable oil cooking spray

4 salmon fillets (approximately 6 ounces each)

1/4 teaspoon salt

1/8 teaspoon freshly ground black pepper

Position a flat broiler pan 6 inches from the source of heat and preheat the broiler.

In a small saucepan, bring the vinegar, ginger, green onion, and garlic to a simmer over low heat. Remove from the heat and set aside.

Meanwhile, spray the broiler pan with nonstick cooking spray. Season the salmon with salt and pepper. Broil the salmon, skin side down, until just opaque when flaked in the center with the tip of a knife, 5 to 7 minutes. Transfer the fish to warmed dinner plates.

Spoon the vinegar with its seasonings over the fish and serve immediately.

Note: The salmon can also be grilled outside. Prepare a fire in a kettle-type charcoal grill. When the coals are hot and turn white, spread them evenly in the bottom of the grill. Lightly oil the grill grate. Place the salmon, skin side down, on the grill grate and cover. Cook until the fish is opaque when flaked in the center, about 5 minutes.

Swordfish and Red Bell Pepper Spiedini
with Balsamic Lemon-Mint Marinade

In Modena, one of the traditional uses for balsamic vinegar is to splash it over grilled fish. This dish combines that tradition with the classic spiedini or kebab. The marinade would also complement tuna, chicken, lamb, or pork.

SERVES 4

Balsamic Lemon-Mint Marinade:

1/4 cup balsamic vinegar

Grated zest of 1 large lemon

1 tablespoon plus 1 teaspoon chopped fresh mint leaves or
*   1 1/2 teaspoons dried mint*

2 garlic cloves, crushed through a press

1/4 teaspoon salt

1/4 teaspoon red pepper flakes

1/2 cup extra virgin olive oil

1 1/2 pounds skinless swordfish, cut into 16 one-inch-square pieces

1 large red bell pepper, stemmed, seeded, and cut into 16 pieces

Balsamic vinegar, for serving

To make the marinade, whisk together all of the ingredients in a medium bowl. Add the swordfish and pepper pieces and toss to coat with the marinade. Let stand for 30 minutes, tossing occasionally. Do not marinate longer, or the vinegar will "cook" the fish and make it firm.

Prepare a fire in a kettle-type charcoal grill. When the coals are hot and turn white, spread them evenly in the bottom of the grill. On four metal skewers, alternately thread 4 swordfish cubes and 4 pepper pieces, reserving the marinade. Grill the spiedini, turning once, until the swordfish is barely cooked through, 6 to 8 minutes. Brush the spiedieni occasionally with the reserved marinade.

To serve, slide the swordfish and peppers off the skewers onto dinner plates. Spoon the remaining marinade over each portion. Pass a cruet of balsamic vinegar.

BROILED CHICKEN THIGHS
WITH HONEY AND BALSAMIC GLAZE

✦

This simple glaze is an easy and quick way to add flavor to a meal. Try it on other grilled poultry
and game. It's especially good on boneless duck breast or quail. In any case, apply the glaze
only during the last 5 minutes of cooking time, or the honey may burn.

SERVES 3 OR 4

8 chicken thighs (approximately 6 ounces each),
    bone in and skin on

2 tablespoons olive oil

1/4 teaspoon salt

1/4 teaspoon freshly ground black pepper

1/4 cup honey

2 tablespoons balsamic vinegar

1 tablespoon chopped fresh sage or 1 1/2 teaspoons dried sage

Position a flat broiler pan or enameled metal baking pan 6 inches from the source of heat and preheat the broiler. Brush the chicken thighs with a little oil and season with salt and pepper.

In a small bowl, whisk the honey, vinegar, and sage together until combined. Set aside.

Broil the chicken, skin side down, until browned, approximately 15 minutes. Turn the chicken and broil until the skin is golden brown and the chicken shows no sign of pink when pierced at a thick part near the bone, 10 to 15 minutes. During the last 5 minutes of cooking, brush the chicken thighs often and liberally with the honey and vinegar mixture, turning the chicken once or twice, until glazed. Serve hot.

GRILLED HERB-RUBBED CHICKEN
DRIZZLED WITH BALSAMIC VINEGAR

❖

Although this marinade is Mediterranean in flavor, its inspiration comes from the Jamaican jerk seasoning technique, where chicken or pork is spread with a wet paste of fresh chopped herbs and spices and left to marinate. Although the paste contains a good hit of balsamic vinegar, serve some extra vinegar at the table to drizzle over the grilled chicken, too.

SERVES 6 TO 8

Herb Paste:

1/2 cup firmly packed fresh basil leaves

1/2 cup chopped fresh parsley

1/4 cup balsamic vinegar

1/4 cup extra virgin olive oil

2 tablespoons Dijon mustard

2 tablespoons chopped fresh rosemary

2 tablespoons chopped fresh thyme

3/4 teaspoon salt

1/4 teaspoon red pepper flakes

Two chickens (approximately 3 1/2 pounds each),
each cut into 8 pieces
Balsamic vinegar, for drizzling

To make the herb paste, in a food processor fitted with the metal blade (or in batches in a blender), pulse all of the ingredients until they resemble a coarse paste.

Place the chicken pieces in a large nonreactive bowl and rub in the paste, coating the chicken completely. Cover and refrigerate for at least 4 hours or up to 24 hours.

Prepare a fire in a kettle-type charcoal grill. Lightly oil the grill grate. When the coals are hot and turn white (leave them in a mound in the center of the grill—do not spread them) arrange the chicken, skin side down, around the cooler outer perimeter of the grate. Cover the grill. Grill the chicken pieces, turning occasionally, until they show no sign of pink when pierced in the thickest part, approximately 45 minutes.

Serve hot or warm, passing a cruet of balsamic vinegar to allow guests to drizzle on the chicken as they wish.

SWEET-AND-SOUR LAMB SHANKS

◆◇◆

In Rome, sweet-and-sour (agrodolce) seasonings find their way into many dishes, particularly meat stews. Onion-smothered lamb shanks are a great way to savor this juxtaposition of flavors. The balsamic vinegar, with its own sweet-and-sour notes, is the perfect addition.

SERVES 4

4 lamb shanks (approximately 1 pound each)

1/2 teaspoon salt, plus more to taste

1/4 teaspoon freshly ground black pepper, plus more to taste

3 tablespoons olive oil

2 yellow onions, cut in half and sliced
    into 1/4-inch-thick half moons

1 tablespoon chopped fresh rosemary or 1 1/2 teaspoons
    dried rosemary

2 large garlic cloves, finely chopped

1 cup dry white wine

3 tablespoons honey

3 tablespoons balsamic vinegar

Preheat the oven to 325 degrees F. Season the lamb shanks with the salt and pepper. In a large heatproof casserole, heat 1 1/2 tablespoons of the oil over medium-high heat. Add half of the lamb and cook, turning occasionally, until browned on all sides, approximately 10 minutes. Repeat with the remaining 1 1/2 tablespoons of oil and lamb. Remove the lamb and pour off all but 2 tablespoons of the fat.

Add the onions and cover. Cook, stirring occasionally, until the onions soften, approximately 5 minutes. Uncover and cook, stirring often, until golden brown, approximately 5 minutes. Add the rosemary and garlic and cook for 1 minute. Add the wine and stir, scraping up any browned bits on the bottom of the casserole. Return the lamb shanks to the casserole and cover tightly.

Bake until the lamb is very tender, 1 hour and 45 minutes to 2 hours. Transfer the lamb to a deep serving platter and cover with aluminum foil to keep warm. Skim off any fat from the surface of the onions. Place the casserole over medium heat and add the honey. Cook, stirring often, until the cooking liquid is reduced and the onions are glazed, approximately 6 minutes. Stir in the vinegar. Season with salt and pepper to taste.

To serve, spoon the onions and juices over the lamb and serve immediately.

FILET MIGNONS

WITH SHALLOT AND BALSAMIC VINEGAR SAUCE

◆

When you want an elegant dinner in a hurry, try this simple dish of filet mignons in a balsamic vinegar sauce. This sauté-and-sauce technique can be adapted to just about any pan-cooked meat, poultry, or fish—it's especially good with lamb chops and boneless chicken breasts. The recipe is easily doubled, just use a larger skillet. (photograph on page 64)

SERVES 2

2 *beef filet mignons (approximately 8 ounces each),*
    cut 1 1/4 inches thick

1/4 *teaspoon salt*

1/8 *teaspoon freshly ground black pepper*

2 *teaspoons olive or vegetable oil*

1 *tablespoon unsalted butter*

1 *tablespoon finely chopped shallot*

1/4 *cup homemade beef broth, or low-sodium canned broth*

2 *tablespoons balsamic vinegar*

Pat the filet mignons dry and season on both sides with the salt and pepper.

In a medium skillet, heat the oil over medium-high heat. Add the filet mignons and cook until the undersides are brown, approximately 3 minutes. Turn and brown the other side, approximately 3 minutes. Reduce the heat to medium and cook until the filets are medium rare, approximately 2 minutes, or until they reach desired doneness. Transfer the filets to a cake rack set over a plate. (The rack helps the filets hold their juices, which would be released if the filets were held on a flat surface, such as a plate.)

Return the skillet to the heat and add the butter and shallot. Cook, stirring almost constantly, until the shallot softens, approximately 1 minute. Add the broth and increase the heat to high. Boil, scraping up the browned bits in the skillet with a wooden spoon, until the broth is reduced to 2 tablespoons, approximately 1 minute. Stir in the vinegar and cook for 30 seconds.

Transfer the filets to warmed dinner plates and pour the sauce over them. Serve immediately.

POT ROAST, ITALIAN-STYLE

This is a pot roast that would make an Italian grandmother proud—tender beef in a rich tomato–red wine sauce thickened with lots of vegetables and garlic and refined with a bit of balsamic vinegar. Serve it with mashed potatoes or pasta to soak up every last drop of the delicious sauce.

SERVES 6 TO 8

3 tablespoons olive oil

One 3-pound beef chuck roast

1 teaspoon salt, plus more to taste

1/4 teaspoon freshly ground black pepper, plus more to taste

1 large onion, thickly sliced

2 carrots, cut into 1/4-inch-thick rounds

2 celery ribs with leaves, cut into 1/4-inch-thick slices

6 garlic cloves, crushed

1 cup dry red wine

1 pound ripe Roma tomatoes, peeled, seeded, and coarsely chopped, or one 16-ounce can peeled tomatoes, chopped, undrained

3 tablespoons balsamic vinegar

Preheat the oven to 325 degrees F. In a large heatproof casserole, heat 1 1/2 tablespoons of the oil over medium-high heat. Season the roast on all sides with the 1 teaspoon salt and 1/4 teaspoon pepper and place in the casserole. Cook, turning once, until browned, approximately 8 minutes. Transfer to a plate.

Add the remaining 1 1/2 tablespoons of oil to the casserole. Add the onions, carrots, celery, and garlic. Reduce the heat to medium and cover. Cook, stirring often, until the vegetables soften, approximately 8 minutes.

Add the red wine and tomatoes and bring to a boil. Cook until slightly reduced, approximately 5 minutes. Return the meat to the casserole and cover. Bake until the meat is fork-tender, approximately 2 hours.

Transfer the meat to a deep serving platter and cover with foil to keep warm. Let the casserole stand off the heat for 5 minutes. Skim off any fat that rises to the surface. Transfer the sauce with the vegetables to a blender or a food processor fitted with the metal blade, add the vinegar, and purée. Season the sauce with salt and pepper to taste. Pour the sauce over the meat and serve immediately. (The pot roast and sauce can be prepared up to 2 days ahead. Let cool, then combine the meat and sauce, cover tightly, and refrigerate. Reheat gently before serving.)

DESSERTS

Vinegar does not usually make its way into the dessert course, but the supple, intensely concentrated sweetness and syrupy quality that characterizes well-aged aceto balsamico tradizionale *lends itself to a short list of* dolci. *In fact, authentic basalmico has a long legacy of being enjoyed at the end of the meal. Century-old balsamico was frequently sipped in small amounts as an after-dinner cordial or mixed with liqueurs to make a digestive. Balsamic vinegar was also appreciated for its sweeter pleasures. In his book,* In Cucina con l'Aceto Balsamico, *balsamic vinegar expert Renato Bergonzini reveals traditional Modenese recipes that call for the precious commodity to be, among other things, mixed into ice cream, sherbets, and custards.*

The desserts in this chapter are only worth making if you use a well-aged artisan-quality balsamico. It should be dark brown and viscous, with jammy, richly layered notes and very little acidity. If the vinegar has a lot of character and density but lacks sweetness, you can cheat and add a pinch of brown sugar. Or you can reduce the vinegar down to a syrup by cooking it in a nonreactive saucepan over medium heat, stirring occasionally.

A fine balsamic vinegar accents the naturally sweet flavors of fresh fruit. Simply drizzled over ice-cold slices of melon or pear, it makes a refreshing summer dessert that requires no advance preparation. For an ethereal treat, do as the Romans and make fragole balsamico *—quartered strawberries tossed with a few drops of aceto balsamico and freshly ground black pepper. For a variation on this classic dessert, try the Lemon-Vanilla Gelato with Raspberries Balsamico. Balsamic vinegar can also be used to enliven a winter fruit salad, by tempering it with a little honey. And if you are fortunate enough to get your hands on an* extra vecchio tradizionale, *pour it over homemade Strawberry Granita.*

FRESH FIGS AND BLACKBERRIES
WITH BALSAMIC MASCARPONE

◆—◆—◆

*This dessert proves that if the cook has excellent ingredients, a dish doesn't have to be time-consuming
to be delicious. Make this blissfully simple recipe when figs and blackberries are at their peak of flavor.
If you can't find mascarpone, substitute 3/4 cup heavy cream whipped with the brown sugar.*

SERVES 6

8 ounces mascarpone cheese

1 tablespoon brown sugar

*1 tablespoon balsamic vinegar, preferably aceto balsamico
    tradizionale*

12 ripe figs, cut lengthwise into quarters

1 cup (1/2 pint) fresh blackberries

In a small bowl, using a rubber spatula, mash the mascarpone with the brown sugar and vinegar until the brown sugar dissolves.

Spoon one-sixth of the mascarpone in the center of each of 6 dessert plates. Arrange 8 fig quarters in a spoke pattern around the edges of the mascarpone, inserting the ends of the figs into the cheese. Sprinkle with a few blackberries. Serve immediately.

FRESH WINTER FRUIT SALAD
WITH BALSAMIC AND HONEY DRESSING

❖

This dessert is perfect for a holiday brunch, when the available fruits may not be exotic or colorful, but are delicious nonetheless. The acid in the vinegar keeps the fruit from turning brown, so the salad can be made a few hours ahead of serving. The dressing is also good on summer fruit salads, especially those that contain berries. Chill this salad at least 1 hour. (photograph on page 86)

SERVES 6; MAKES 3/4 CUP DRESSING

1/2 cup honey

1/4 cup balsamic vinegar

2 ripe Bartlett pears, preferably red, unpeeled, cored, and cut into 1/2-inch-thick wedges

2 Granny Smith apples, unpeeled, cored, and cut into 1/2-inch-thick wedges

2 seedless clementines or other sweet mandarins, peeled and separated into segments

2 cups seedless grapes (red, green, or a combination)

3/4 cup pomegranate seeds (from approximately 1/2 pomegranate; see Note)

In a medium bowl, whisk the honey and vinegar until combined. Add the pears, apples, clementines, grapes, and pomegranate seeds and toss to coat the fruit completely with the honey mixture. Cover and refrigerate for 1 hour or up to 6 hours. Serve chilled.

Note: To remove the seeds from pomegranates without becoming stained with juice, first cut the fruit through the stem end, stopping halfway down. Fill a large bowl or sink with cold water and submerge the fruit completely. Working under water, break open the fruit to divide into quarters and reveal the seeds. Remove the seeds, which will sink to the bottom. Discard the bitter pith and the thick skins. Drain the seeds.

LEMON-VANILLA GELATO
WITH RASPBERRIES BALSAMICO

⬥

Intrepid gourmets can find first-class ice cream in gelaterias all over Italy, but only the very best restaurants serve gelato sprinkled with a few drops of high-quality balsamico. This unlikely combination is heaven-sent, but use the best balsamic vinegar you can find. Note that the gelato must freeze for at least 4 hours. (photograph on page 87)

SERVES 4 TO 6
MAKES APPROXIMATELY 1 QUART GELATO:

3 cups half-and-half or light cream

3/4 cup sugar

Zest of 1 small lemon, removed with a vegetable peeler

1/2 vanilla bean, split lengthwise, or 1/2 teaspoon vanilla extract

6 large egg yolks

1 cup (1/2 pint) fresh raspberries

Balsamic vinegar, for serving

In a medium, heavy-bottomed saucepan, combine the half-and-half, sugar, lemon zest, and vanilla bean. Bring to a simmer over medium-low heat, stirring often. Remove from the heat.

In a medium bowl, whisk the egg yolks until thick and light colored. Gradually whisk in approximately 1 cup of the hot half-and-half mixture. Slowly whisk the egg mixture into the saucepan. Cook over low heat, stirring constantly with a wooden spoon, until the custard is thick enough to coat the spoon, 3 to 5 minutes (an instant-read thermometer inserted in the custard should read 180 degrees F.). Immediately strain the custard into a medium bowl set in a larger bowl of ice water. Remove the vanilla bean. Using the tip of a sharp knife, scrape the seeds from the bean into the custard, and discard the bean. Let stand until the custard is chilled, stirring often, approximately 15 minutes.

Transfer the custard to the container of an ice cream maker and process according to the manufacturer's directions. Pack the gelato into a freezer container, cover tightly, and freeze for at least 4 hours before serving. (The gelato is best if served within 2 days.)

To serve, spoon the gelato into chilled dessert bowls and top with raspberries. Serve immediately with a cruet of balsamic vinegar, allowing each guest to drizzle the gelato with the vinegar to taste.

STRAWBERRY GRANITA

Granitas are icy frozen fruit desserts closely related to sorbets. Whereas sorbets are churned in ice cream machines until smooth, granitas need no special equipment — they are frozen in a pan to achieve the desired coarse texture. The combination of fresh strawberries and balsamic vinegar has been cherished by the cooks of Modena for years. This is a refreshing twist on that pairing, and makes an excellent late spring dessert. To do it justice, seek out the finest balsamic vinegar. Note that the granita needs about 3 hours to freeze.

MAKES APPROXIMATELY 1 QUART; SERVES 4 TO 6

2 pints fresh strawberries, hulled and sliced

1 cup sugar

2 tablespoons fresh lemon juice

Balsamic vinegar, for serving

Place a 9- by 13-inch nonreactive metal pan and a large metal spoon in a freezer and chill for 15 minutes.

In a food processor fitted with the metal blade, process the strawberries, sugar, and lemon juice until coarsely puréed, approximately 15 seconds. Pour into the chilled pan. Freeze until the mixture is semi-solid and icy around the edges, approximately 1 hour. Use the cold spoon to chop and mash and mix the icy edges into the center. Freeze until the edges are icy again, approximately 1 hour. Repeat the mixing procedure. Freeze until the mixture is completely frozen and icy, but still soft enough to scoop, approximately 1 hour. (If the mixture freezes solid, break into large pieces, transfer to a food processor fitted with the metal blade, and pulse until coarsely chopped.)

Scoop into chilled dessert bowls. Serve immediately with a cruet of balsamic vinegar, allowing each guest to drizzle the granita with vinegar to taste.

METRIC CONVERSIONS

LIQUID WEIGHTS

U.S. Measurements	Metric Equivalents
1/4 teaspoon	1.23 ml
1/2 teaspoon	2.5 ml
3/4 teaspoon	3.7 ml
1 teaspoon	5 ml
1 dessertspoon	10 ml
1 tablespoon (3 teaspoons)	15 ml
2 tablespoons (1 ounce)	30 ml
1/4 cup	60 ml
1/3 cup	80 ml
1/2 cup	120 ml
2/3 cup	160 ml
3/4 cup	180 ml
1 cup (8 ounces)	240 ml
2 cups (1 pint)	480 ml
3 cups	720 ml
4 cups (1 quart)	1 liter
4 quarts (1 gallon)	3 3/4 liters

DRY WEIGHTS

U.S. Measurements	Metric Equivalents
1/4 ounce	7 grams
1/3 ounce	10 grams
1/2 ounce	14 grams
1 ounce	28 grams
1 1/2 ounces	42 grams
1 3/4 ounces	50 grams
2 ounces	57 grams
3 ounces	85 grams
3 1/2 ounces	100 grams
4 ounces (1/4 pound)	114 grams
6 ounces	170 grams
8 ounces (1/2 pound)	227 grams
9 ounces	250 grams
16 ounces (1 pound)	464 grams

TEMPERATURES

Fahrenheit	Celsius (Centigrade)
32°F (water freezes)	0°C
200°F	95°C
212°F (water boils)	100°C
250°F	120°C
275°F	135°C
300°F (slow oven)	150°C
325°F	160°C
350°F (moderate oven)	175°C
375°F	190°C
400°F (hot oven)	205°C
425°F	220°C
450°F (very hot oven)	230°C
475°F	245°C
500°F (extremely hot oven)	260°C

LENGTH

U.S. Measurements	Metric Equivalents
1/8 inch	3 mm
1/4 inch	6 mm
3/8 inch	1 cm
1/2 inch	1.2 cm
3/4 inch	2 cm
1 inch	2.5 cm
1 1/4 inches	3.1 cm
1 1/2 inches	3.7 cm
2 inches	5 cm
3 inches	7.5 cm
4 inches	10 cm
5 inches	12.5 cm

APPROXIMATE EQUIVALENTS

1 kilo is slightly more than 2 pounds
1 liter is slightly more than 1 quart
1 meter is slightly over 3 feet
1 centimeter is approximately 3/8 inch

MAIL-ORDER SOURCES FOR BALSAMIC VINEGAR

❖❖❖

The following list of specialty retailers sell artisan-made and good-quality commercial balsamic vinegars.
For additional sources, seek out fine food stores in your area that specialize in Italian products.

Balducci's
424 Sixth Avenue, New York, NY 10011
(212) 673-2600, (800) 225-3822
Catalog available

Bristol Farms Market
606 Fair Oaks Avenue, South Pasadena, CA 91030
(818) 441-5450

Convito Italiano
1515 Sheridan Road, Wilmette, IL 60091
(708) 251-3654

Corti Brothers
5810 Folsom Boulevard, Sacramento, CA 95819
(916) 736-3800
Catalog available

De Medici Importers Limited
214 North Main Street, Florida, NY 10921
(914) 651-4400

Dean & DeLuca
560 Broadway, New York, NY 10012
(800) 221-7714, (212) 431-1691
Catalog available

Draeger's
342 First Street, Los Altos, CA 94022
(415) 948-4425
and
1010 University Drive, Menlo Park, CA 94025
(415) 688-0677

The Mozzarella Company
2944 Elm Street, Dallas, TX 75226
(800) 798-2954, (214) 741-4072
Catalog available

Rogers' International Limited
44 Taunton Lake Drive, Newtown, CT 06470-1518
(203) 426-0216

Todaro Brothers
555 Second Avenue, New York, NY 10016
(212) 679-7766
Catalog available

Vivande Porta Via
2125 Fillmore Street, San Francisco, CA 94115
(415) 346-4430
Catalog available

Williams-Sonoma
100 North Point, San Francisco, CA 94133
(800) 541-2233
Catalogue available

Zingerman's
422 Detroit Street, Ann Arbor, Michigan 48104
(313) 663-DELI
Catalogue available

Importer and distributor of vinegar casks
for master cooper Francesco Renzi of Modena:

Paul Bertolli
39 Alamo Avenue, Berkeley, CA 94708-1327
(510) 526-7041

INDEX